How to Transform Your Company

and Enjoy It

D0807509

How to Transform Your Company and Enjoy It

Ken Lewis
and
Stephen Lytton

2000

First edition published in 1995 by Management Books 2000 Ltd

This new edition published in 1997 by Management Books 2000 Ltd
Cowcombe House
Cowcombe Hill
Chalford
Gloucestershire GL6 8HP
Tel: 01285 760722
FAX 01285 760708
E-Mail: MB2000@compuserve.com

Illustrations by Jed Pascoe

Printed and bound in Great Britain by Astron On-Line, Letchworth

British Library Cataloguing in Publication Data is available

ISBN 1-85252-222-4

Acknowledgements

As a host company to the Department of Trade and Industry's *Inside UK Enterprise*, Dutton Engineering has frequent visitors, some genuinely seeking to find out just how we are achieving what we are, some perhaps hopeful of finding some chink in our armour and secretly hoping that we will fall flat on our faces. You'd be amazed how many excuses we hear in our session discussions about the reasons given for just why such practices won't work in their particular company or organisation – 'Our industry is different.'; 'My Board members would all have heart attacks.'; 'This might work in a small company, but ours is so much larger.'

All these remarks are probably true to a greater or lesser extent, but somehow one is nevertheless left with the feeling that the comments are not so much reasons, but rather excuses for keeping things the same, for not changing. Perhaps it is that the comment comes from a non-board director or a senior manager rendered powerless by a tyrannical chief executive or that their company culture has brought about such antagonistic relations with the workforce that it will take years to reconstruct a genuine customer-focused operation.

5

There can be no doubt that, where change is concerned, opportunity, resources and the power to act are essential. No less important is support and encouragement, and it is here that I must acknowledge the help and firm support of many in helping bring to fruition this book – my contribution to the competitiveness debate of how to take the UK back into the forefront of world manufacturing.

To my collaborator on this book, Steve Lytton, Network Co-ordinator of the Central Logistics Association for Supply-Chain Partnerships (CLASP), our local supply-chain network group, encompassing Bedfordshire and North Bucks, I would like to express my thanks for encouraging me to get the Dutton experience down on paper, for his editing skills and valuable contributions to the text, and for ensuring that the book would actually be published.

Among those others to whom I owe greatest thanks are my colleague Tina Mason, for her constant reminders about just how we did things and for her overall input; and our one-time secretary, Isobel Keech, for all the transcription work.

A special word of thanks go to Jed Pascoe, the cartoonist, whose artistic skills, humour and imagination have helped bring my presentations alive and convey the Dutton message to many hundreds of business people in the UK and abroad.

Our suppliers and customers also deserve a strong mention here. As the book reveals, our success is bound up with theirs and vice versa. I am confident that their perception of our journey will not be too far removed from what has been written here.

Almost finally, I would like to express the warmest thanks and regards to all current and ex-members of staff of Dutton Engineering (Woodside) Ltd. What we have achieved, and are continuing to achieve, in the difficult economic circumstances of the UK economy is a testimony to their wisdom and commitment to Dutton, as well as to the degree of trust that we have managed to build up among us over the years. All of what appears in this book is a result of our joint efforts. Having seen our joint vision slowly take shape before my eyes, I am confident that they will want these experiences to be widely shared, if only to prove that better ways of doing things exist than the conventional adversarial way. I know that what we have at Dutton is special, but not so special that it cannot be spread.

Lastly, for those other chief executives and managers who come to embrace the challenge of change in a similar way as us and eventually come to find renewed fun and satisfaction at work, let me send my greetings and say just one thing. When you've got something good to pass on, just do it; don't hang on to it. We all benefit in the end.

Ken Lewis
Dutton Engineering (Woodside) Ltd

Contents

9

Foreword to paperback edition

Since this book was first published in 1995, we have come across several other companies, both much larger and of similar size, in which many of the practices we are using at Dutton are becoming an ever-strengthening part of their own corporate fabric. This, we believe, lends increasing credence to the value of the approach adopted at Dutton. In a period when the sand seems to be shifting increasingly rapidly, it is most reassuring to see others embarking on their own journeys in a similar way to ourselves, and to learn that they are also experiencing the same kind of tangible benefits.

It also reaffirms our view that, though the people making up the workforce at Dutton are remarkable, they are no more remarkable than those making up the workforces of other visionary companies elsewhere within the UK and abroad. What marks off these people and their companies is their preparedness to take a chance, to commit, and to follow a clear lead. That is where Senior Management comes in - providing the resources, the encouragement and the vision. As the competition continues to hot up, this job is even more necessary than before!

Introduction

If it were true that the old ways are the best ways, how is it
that everyone is looking for new ways?

For today's managers, change and challenge are the order
of the day. The pace is such that, for many, the situation
appears way out of control. The response of some is to seek
to return to rigid control systems, but, like it or not, with the
competition after us at every turn, future survival will
depend not on the old but on new ways of thinking and new
organisational forms. What may once have appeared as
radical or revolutionary nowadays represents a positive and
necessary stage towards finally severing the ties of complacency. In this race, no one will survive if they run having tied
their own shoelaces together.

We at Dutton Engineering (Woodside) changed direction
and embarked on the path towards excellence in 1989, having
seen the new ways working successfully at one of our
customers. For us their philosophy of Total Quality
Management came as quite a shock. We had to grasp the
notion that we had internal, as well as external, customers,
and to appreciate that everyone working for the company is
extremely talented and has much to contribute to its success.

13

This shattered the traditional view: that the role of management is to scrutinise data and exercise control in the minutest detail! It is this obsession with small day-to-day transactions that prevents managers from being visionary and from generating an overall sense of direction within their organisation.

So, what was it that motivated a small company employing 25 people to afford the time and effort required to work towards changing their business practices – a change that challenges 200 years of tradition in the UK? The fact is, and remains, that we had absolutely no choice in the matter. We could no longer afford not to change.

My view is that this state of affairs now applies to UK industry as a whole. Something must be done. In the words of the late Dr Deming: 'Survival is not compulsory.' If we hope or intend to maintain our living standards in the West, the past small increases in performance of the magnitude of 2 per cent, 5 per cent, or even 10 per cent, will not be enough. We are going to need improvements of 30 per cent, 50 per cent and even 100 per cent. To achieve this we are going to have to change and ensure that those around us change too.

We are, moreover, going to have to ensure that our shareholders provide not only the resources but also the time for this to happen. This is not a quick fix, but a journey taking several years. So, who is going to have to change? Not least the shareholders, who will have to come to terms with the fact that it will be the people on the shop floor who will have a major role to play in the turnaround.

It is often said that North American, UK and European shareholders have the reputation for being somewhat thrusting and predatory. Like in everything, there is clearly a degree of truth in this. But we must not lose sight of the fact that a large percentage of these shareholders are pension fund holders whose brief is, at least in part, to look after our long-term interests. Such people must also come to share the vision. But, as always, what is absolutely vital is support from the top.

Experience has shown that of the companies that embark on the Total Quality route, only 20 per cent actually achieve any lasting success. Thus, there can be no room for vacillation in the boardroom. Total Quality Management is about the continual and unceasing reduction of waste, and this can only be achieved and sustained through the elimination of the barriers and controls set up by management.

So, what is the role of senior management in all this? It is simply to set out and promote a vision, and to cascade that vision effectively through the whole of the organisation. It means believing in what you say and not merely mouthing the words. People will respect and respond to sincerity. Empty words will achieve nothing. The issue at stake is thorough-going cultural change. This demands courage, and senior management has to be brave.

A review of the present situation in UK industry shows that many middle managers have risen to their present positions on the merit of their technical abilities and seniority, not because of those all-important people skills. Such colleagues tend, understandably, to defend their areas stoutly, and may find it difficult to pass the responsibility down the line and empower their colleagues. I am convinced that the skills required by managers today are precisely those of being a leader, a coach and a facilitator. With the right teams of people around you, properly motivated and all facing in the same direction, the goal of becoming a world-class manufacturer or organisation is within everyone's reach – providing they themselves believe it can be done.

The Dangers of Complacency

In the past, the Western countries have tended to view their hitherto commercial superiority with a considerable degree of complacency. But life has now caught up, and, on our small planet and with the development of technology and instant communications, the advantages previously enjoyed have been steadily eroded. Globalisation has meant that business, and indeed manufacture, can easily be conducted in virtually any corner of the world. Large international companies can switch parts of their operations, not merely from town to town or from country to country, but even from continent to continent in their search to maintain a competitive edge. This role of being a big player on the world stage must be kept uppermost in our minds if we are to keep money, jobs and manufacturing alive in the UK. Even where we ourselves are not directly exporting, doubtless we supply someone who is. And, meanwhile, the competition, much of it from the Pacific Rim countries, continues to snap at our heels.

'How,' one might ask, 'are we to compete on this world stage confronted by the absurdly low labour rates in these emerging countries?' The challenge to business is precisely this: how can companies remain commercially profitable, while striving to attain world-class performance?

In my experience, the solution lies in the ceaseless reduction of waste: wasted time, wasted materials, wasted effort. I can assure you that it is possible to drive down the costs of running your business while lifting quality and performance levels. In my view, the achievable savings could be as much as the equivalent of 20-30 per cent of annual sales!

One thing is clear: even in the tough times of the early 1980s – a period in which our world has changed beyond all recognition, forcing new ways of trading and organisation, a period in which, for most people, the daily news consisted of closures, upturns, downturns and U-turns, and the icy blast of redundancies, downsizing and now rightsizing – nevertheless, some companies, some organisations, and some people not only survived, but survived well and prospered.

This book is about one of those companies, Dutton Engineering (Woodside), my company, which has not only weathered the storm, but has in fact gone from strength to strength. Formed as a subcontract sheet metal working company in 1972, Dutton, along with the rest, experienced the rollercoaster change of fortune that beset the UK economy. In 1983, we successfully completed a management buyout, and during the last six to ten years I have presided, as Managing Director, over a whole programme of re-engineering within the company.

Among the decisive elements was the re-engineering of myself as a manager. This meant relinquishing what might be perceived as some of traditional management's most closely coveted privileges. However, what I lost was more than compensated for by the gains. I am now a far richer character with a greater vocabulary, embracing the terms *Kaizen*, *Kanban*, Just in Time (JIT), Statistical Process Control (SPC), Total Quality Management (TQM) and Business Excellence. But, most importantly, besides seeing my own attitudes change, I have also seen those of my colleagues around me change, too. Like a ripple, the change has spread, enhancing the quality of all our lives. This is a goal well worth striving for.

And what about the effect on the company? Throughout the recession of the 1990s, my company has continued to grow its sales year on year. True, we were fortunate in having benefited from the niche market of stainless-steel fabrications, and as such had a slight advantage over some other small companies. However, in such complex times, small advantages tend to disappear all too rapidly, and, since change was in the air, we had no real choice but to go for it.

The lessons we have learnt on our journey towards Business Excellence are not relevant to us alone. They are appropriate to all companies, and it is precisely this fact and the dire straits of UK manufacturing today that prompted me to go into print.

However, before describing our path, I must dispel the myth that your own 'journey to excellence' need cost you a small fortune. You will not have to hire expensive armies of consultants, nor will you need to start writing out cheques for plant, equipment, etc. The change process at Dutton was, and is, being accomplished without the necessity for any large financial investment, and I am confident that, for most companies, the same will prove true.

In the early years, the real investment will be in training everyone in your organisation to understand their own role in your company's success. The focus of change will be on changing the traditional attitudes and control systems held by management, breaking down the barriers and unleashing the potential of each individual employee. This will be a daunting challenge to senior management. It is rather like standing on the side of a lake of unknown temperature and depth. Should one just dip one's toe in or should one dive straight in? I would urge and encourage you to be brave. Dive in. I can assure you the water's lovely.

1

Why Change? For Change We Must!

Change can certainly be unsettling. It makes people justifiably apprehensive of what might happen, not only to their company, but also to themselves personally. Except when crisis – often financial – threatens, there is usually a common and understandable reluctance to rock the boat. However, nowadays, in times of change and chaos, it no longer matters how good you actually are. What matters is how good your customers perceive you to be. Expectations are very different from those of five or ten years ago.

Today, customers demand quality goods, delivered on time, and they want continuing cost reductions into the bargain. They demand greater choice, while all the time seeking to reduce their own financial burden by holding minimum stocks. But what do these changes actually represent? And how is it that these demands have proved so difficult to meet?

My view is that we have often struggled because we considered that the only way to cope with change was to spend more money doing the same things, only better. In the past, the great salvation has been seen as technology, and for some organisations this remains the case. Computerisation and automation were hailed as the universal panacea. Huge investments in time and money were laid at the altar of technology, and yet the goals remained as elusive as ever. Moreover, many of these wonderful technological marvels have proved to be masters rather than servants, often because the financial investment was so great that any criticism would have led to the charge of heresy. Many directors have tended to think that any problem could be solved if enough money were spent on the latest plant or equipment. Some have maintained this view even when the reverse has proved to be the case.

The fact is that we are rarely getting the maximum out of the machinery that we have already got. And the reason for this has tended to be completely missed. It is that we have generally neglected the most fundamental and valuable of our assets – the talents of the people we employ. Despite the view of certain hardened cynics out there, human beings do not actually become obsolete and worn out like machine tools and computers. They are infinitely versatile, resourceful and innovative. They are able to perform miracles with existing machinery, tools and systems.

It is here – by tapping into the great energies and resourcefulness of the people within our organisations – that we can fundamentally begin to address our customers' requirements.

Historically, Britain's working environment has been hierarchically structured. Management has come to believe its role is to place its ideas and wisdom into the hands of those who actually carry out the production or the processes that occur within their organisations. Such notions belong very much in the past. Where such attitudes prevail, fundamental progress is not possible.

The key to successful change is empowerment and in getting the workforce to comprehend very deeply that they are recognised, respected and appreciated as a very valuable resource for the organisation. After all, it is these people that actually are the front-line shock troops. It is they who will be driving out the waste from within the organisation, who will identify and remove the non-added value activities. This is a task that can only be done effectively by the people who play an active part in the day-to-day processes.

All this is clear: every employee is the expert in terms of his or her sphere of activity. Given the right motivation and genuine empowerment, these people will bring forth ideas and improvements that touch every aspect of company life. Too often we waste our colleagues' talents by keeping them focused on hierarchical relationships and obliging them to look upwards for instructions. The inescapable fact is that management does not have all the answers.

Such issues are at the heart of the drive for Total Quality. But what actually is this elusive quality that so many are striving for but never reaching? Quality is embodied in a Rolls Royce, but could not a Mini also be perceived as quality? Surely, quality is that which is embodied in a product or service that totally satisfies the customer's requirements. Quality goes far beyond quality assurance and inspection departments.

At Dutton, quality touches every single aspect of the company's activities. It includes quality of information, quality improvements and the quality of change. Quality must be integral to every activity that you do within your company, and, as you start to measure the costs of poor quality, such areas become a focus for improvement.

In my company, measurement was certainly a key tool as we started our drive for excellence. And, as with our company, once everyone in your organisation understands what quality really means, and what their personal role in it is, you will notice the natural evolution of highly dynamic, cross-functional teams. It is your staff (your colleagues) who will steadily eliminate the waste generated within your business (and theirs) – waste which will otherwise hold it back, waste which will prevent genuine competitiveness and which may very well come to pose a real threat to its actual survival.

2

Cultural Change – A Lesson Learnt

Over the last 50 years we have seen a radical shift of industrial and economic power from the well-developed Western countries to the Far Eastern countries, and to Japan in particular. In my view, much of this shift is a result of the fundamental difference in the perception of quality held by the West and the East.

History paints a picture of considerable diversity, and much can be understood from looking back so as to grasp how things have come to be as they are and why the issue of quality has been interpreted so differently. In previous times, while Japan was still leading a very isolated existence, the Western countries were venturing forth and building up empires. This period encouraged rapid growth in terms of the ability to communicate instructions over great distances through the development of the networks of diplomatic channels and the highly successful commercial operations of companies such as the British East India Company.

Interestingly, it was precisely this company that produced

one of the first management books, although the subject matter was not concerned with management per se. The topic was the breaking and training of horses. The company produced a fully comprehensive instruction manual, which helped produce consistent quality in terms of the breeding and training of horses throughout their large organisation.

The success of this manual inspired them further. They then sought to develop standards of training among the indigenous peoples who were working for the company, and similar procedures were published for the management of these particular areas of their operations. It is here that we can detect some of the earliest, rigid influences that remain with us today.

At this time, the backbone of all the European nations was still the village and small town economy, which under-pinned these countries' expansion. Commercially, life was based around village artisans, such as the blacksmith. The blacksmith knew exactly what his customers wanted, under-stood what they were prepared to pay, and would deliver the goods on time. He would also continually develop new ideas and innovative equipment to improve both his own perfor-mance, and that of his customers. He would be training and motivating his small staff of apprentices. As early as those times, tightly structured methods of control were being developed to achieve results. Over the last 400 or so years, it was customers who led the requirements, with the softer, human issues running in parallel.

Some friends of mine who used to work in the aircraft industry before the Second World War have told me that they can still relate to this village scenario, since it was still very prevalent within their industry even then. Aircraft were usually built one at a time, with no two exactly the same. Although built to perform to the customers' exact specifications, these aircraft were nevertheless constructed by very skilled craftsmen, who were always looking for ways to improve their processes and expertise.

However, with the outbreak of war and the increasing number of aircraft required, the old methods of production ceased to be appropriate. Small satellite factories were created to cope with the demand and to take up the influx of unskilled labour. Faced by the necessity of ensuring that reliable equipment was available to the Armed Forces, the Ministry of Defence (MoD) and aircraft organisations rapidly had to develop inspection criteria and quality control procedures. It was out of these, and the MoD enquiry in 1945 as to why half the bombs dropped on Germany had failed to explode, that BS 5750 (now ISO 9000) eventually came into being in 1979 for industry and commerce.

In 1984, having spent a full year in preparation, we applied for and obtained the standard BS 5750 Part 2 certification. At the time, I recognised within it the methodology and procedures typical of the defence industry's way of thinking. This gave me quite some concern for the future: if this was the vehicle to which the Government was hitching its hopes of improving the economic performance of the UK, well! However, the time was as it was, and one has to try to understand what motivations lay behind it all. This was the only way forward that was deemed appropriate for the early 1980s.

At Dutton, we were nevertheless very proud of our achievement, and we hung our certificate, number 168, on the wall. Back in the early 1980s, the standard was very new indeed and none of our suppliers or customers really knew much about it at that time. Nowadays, it is seen as an almost obligatory item on customers' approved vendor status lists, and, in fact, many companies now only do business with ISO 9000-approved suppliers. Personally, however, I remained unconvinced that this piece of paper was going to stop my competitors in their tracks.

During that period, many things were in the process of change, and yet, as is so often the case, it was a small thing in my personal life that came to influence my future direction most profoundly.

In the early 1980s, I used to own a black-and-white Ferguson television set, which, over the years, kept breaking down. It was forever being sent back for repair, to the great frustration of the family. As soon as I could, in 1983, I bought my first colour television. This television was manufactured in Japan, and it certainly was not cheap to buy. But, to the family's amazement (and delight) it continued to work faultlessly. In fact it performed perfectly for over 10 years without ever breaking down.

It was from this simple experience that I began to understand why it was that we, in the UK, had been steadily losing our car industry, our motorcycle industry, and now our television industry to the Japanese. Something very dynamic was obviously happening there. After all, before the Second World War the Japanese had hardly been known for producing quality products, and yet there they were with this amazing competitive edge.

I am a great believer in seeing things for myself, and so I decided that I had to visit Japan and find out just how they had been able to achieve such remarkable progress in the areas of quality and reliability.

So, in 1985, I went to Japan with a group of other business people, and had an opportunity to visit companies of all sizes, from mighty Nissan down to small, sheet-metal-working companies. After the three-week visit – a relatively short time to try to understand the whole picture – I came away having learnt what I believe is a fundamental lesson:

the Japanese actually trusted each other. First, the people on the shop floor trusted their management. The management, in turn, trusted the people on the shop floor. More amazingly, they trusted their suppliers. And, more amazing still, they even trusted their customers! What a difference from the position in the UK at that time.

What particularly shook me occurred one Saturday morning, when we were visiting a television factory. Here we saw employees who had come in to put right television sets that they had manufactured wrongly during the week. And they were not even being paid for it. This virtually floored me. I was much more used to paying people to do things wrong, and paying them again to put them right – often on overtime rates.

Over dinner that evening at the hotel the conversation of our British management team was focused on trying to comprehend how all this was possible. There were a variety of possible explanations, but our ultimate conclusion was that trust figured very highly and that a very different kind of relationship existed between management and production operatives. It was apparent that quality was being built into the products, rather than defects being inspected out.

Part of the answer to how this arose can be found by looking at the work of the quality gurus, who were very much instrumental in helping establish Japan's post-war economic recovery and development.

One of the biggest names is that of an American, the late Dr W Edwards Deming. Deming was an erstwhile American government statistician specialising in artillery equipment, for whom recognition among his fellow countrymen only occurred in 1982 when NBC covered the competitive success of the Japanese and the damage they had inflicted on American export markets.

The background to this is as follows. In 1950, when the United Nations, with a large American contingent, were fighting the North Koreans for control of South Korea, huge costs and vast amounts of time were being incurred in bringing munitions all the way from America's industrial heartland over to the South Korean ports.

One solution advanced was to look at Japan as a possible manufacturing centre for munitions. However, after the Second World War, although the majority of the Japanese factories had remained structurally intact, Japan did not have the kind of reputation for reliable and high-quality products that is vital for munitions work. Several specialists, Deming included, were sent to Japan to see whether they could bring product reliability, quality and cost-effectiveness into the munitions production.

Dr Deming spent many long hours with the top Japanese management, who were ready, willing and eager to learn. They were also prepared to be open-minded and to tackle things in a more radical way. The rest is history, but it came as somewhat of a shock for the American people to realise that it had been an American who had been so instrumental in getting the Japanese economy moving so powerfully forward to the envied position it holds today.

Deming is still venerated in Japan today, and is honoured each year through the presentation of the prestigious Deming award to the most-outstanding industrial or commercial organisation in the country. Deming's 14 points for success have been well publicised, and need no further explanation here. However, it is well worth mentioning that the criteria are very people-orientated, and that it is, to my mind, precisely these areas that dominate in the East. Somehow, it appears that Western management is having much greater difficulties coming to terms with the people issues than the Japanese.

The following two quotes make the point clearly. The first is by Dr Albrecht, Chairman of TQS Group.

'The ISO 9000 and BS 5750 approach is a ticket to mediocrity, not to competitive excellence. At its worst it is a slavish belief in the superiority of diagrams and manuals over human intelligence. At its best it does little more than force people to spend more time thinking about the processes than about getting the work done. There are better ways, and they all rely on mobilising the intelligence of all the workers in the company.'

The second is from a *Daily Telegraph* article entitled 'Growth sacrificed to the great British cult of the individual'.

'Perhaps the most haunting words in the RSA report came from a speech made just before Mrs Thatcher came to power by the Japanese industrialist Kanoko Masusi to American business people. "We are going to win, and the industrialised West is going to lose out. There is nothing you can do about it because the reasons for your failure are within yourselves. With your bosses doing the thinking, while the workers wield the screwdrivers, you are convinced deep down that this is the right way to do business. For you the essence of management is getting the ideas out of the heads of the bosses and into the hands of the labour. For us the core of management is the art of mobilising and putting together the intellectual resources of all the employees in the service of the firm".'

I think that, in the last few years, the Western world has at last begun to wake up to the importance of change. We, in the UK, have now adopted the UK Quality Model, where only 14 per cent of the Model is devoted to processes. This

14 per cent is covered very well by ISO 9000. However, this leaves us with the remaining 86 per cent of other issues. It is these that we need to address in a systematic way if we are to get anywhere near our companies and organisations performing to world-class standards. We shall return to the UK and European Model for Total Quality Management later.

Now to the future and what we need to do. As senior managers in our organisations, we have the responsibility of developing a new work ethic within our companies. In my case, I had to completely re-engineer my way of thinking about values, controls, constraints, and the master/servant employee relationship that has been with us for centuries.

These have to be replaced by trust, openness, fairness and by encouraging genuine involvement by everyone within the organisation. We will need to understand what motivates people to work, and what will motivate them in the future. Management can influence the process by evolving a new approach to employee education and rewards. We have to learn how to remove barriers and to allow people to do a good job. We need to allow our colleagues to bring all their skills and expertise to the party. Management in its changed role must understand that they must be leaders, coaches and facilitators.

So, how did we, at Dutton Engineering, get started down this road? And what mistakes were made and successes enjoyed? I believe that the following will contain some lessons for you, the reader, to take on board. By sharing our experiences, we, at Dutton, hope that you will not have to reinvent the wheel.

3

The Dutton Way

I have already described my disappointment at the results we had obtained from pursuing a BS 5750 policy, and also my remarkable visit to Japan in 1985 (Figure 1), where I learnt that trust had a large part to play in the success of the

Figure 1

Japanese economy. Their ability to produce high-quality goods and services consistently with a zero defect rate was quite astounding.

One of my Japanese colleagues told me the following story to illustrate just how seriously quality was taken in Japan. He said that any supplier to a large Japanese corporation, upon sending anything that was not correct to specification or delivered on time, would have their senior manager summoned to the customer's presidential suite to explain the reasons for the failure. Even in the absence of the Samurai sword, the experience was a most salutary one and testified to the passion that needs to exist throughout the organisation in order to achieve the company's goals.

Figure 2

In the West, we have heard about presidents and workforce dressing the same, doing early morning exercises, and singing company songs. This is not the way that we do things here. What this does represent, and what we share at Dutton (and what, furthermore, in my view, all companies need for success), is that all members of the company should be facing in the same direction (Figure 2). At Dutton we are all heading west; those who were facing east have now all gone their separate ways.

Another factor we share with the Japanese is that we reward our employees' contributions to our success with a share in the company's profits. After all, there is a limit to how much effort and enthusiasm you can expect from your colleagues if they do not receive some form of recognition or reward. Our decision has been to reward employees based on 'bottom-line' profitability. This encourages everyone to participate in cost-saving and efficiency improvements throughout the organisation.

Nowadays, we also organise financial courses for the staff so that they can understand a balance sheet and thus know what they are seeing if they wish to look at the Accounts. All this helps breed an atmosphere of trust.

When I returned from my trip to Japan, full of enthusiasm for change and eager to try out some of the ideas I had seen, I was still confronted, of course, with the British way of doing things (Figure 3). It was very much dog-eat-dog,

Figure 3

arm's-length trading, no trust, and a win/lose situation for most people. How frustrated I felt to know that there was a better way of doing business and not knowing how to get there (I call the years from 1985 to 1988 'my blue period'). True, we continued to develop our company, but we consistently had problems with late deliveries. We had inspection departments, but still had quality problems. Our commercial performance was still relatively poor, and who was paying for all this? Our customers! But, at that time, customers were prepared to pay.

What a changed world we live in today! Customers are now demanding quality products, delivered on time, with a large amount of choice, and all the while with minimum stock holding. Furthermore, they now expect year-on-year price reductions!

Domino UK Ltd Set the Pace

In 1988, Domino, a customer with whom we had been working for eight years, invited all their suppliers to attend a company-wide Quality Awareness Day (Figure 4). Domino – developers and manufacturers of high-speed ink-jet printers and one of the more successful Cambridge companies – had introduced into their company a Total Quality Management Programme in 1985, and they were, by then, ready to cascade this philosophy down into their supply chain.

At that time, Domino had some 250 suppliers, and it took them two full days to process them all through their awareness programme. They then offered to help any of their suppliers introduce a Total Quality Management philosophy into their own organisations. Out of the 250 suppliers, only Dutton Engineering took them up on their offer!

Figure 4

This philosophy of TQM had some rather strange notions that took some getting used to. One such was that of the internal customer; another that quality is to do with everybody in the organisation and not merely the concern of the inspection or quality control departments. Most of us had been brought up with the idea that quality was all about the products that you made and sold, the main thing being whether or not it met the customer's specification. Questions such as how to delight the customer and looking at the company holistically took a lot of thinking through.

It took us a whole year of preparation before Dutton was ready to launch its own programme (Figure 5). I decided on a big-bang launch, to emphasise that something really different was going on, and this proved well worthwhile, despite the cost of a day's lost production. As a result, the employees realised we were actually serious about the programme, and prepared to spend time, effort and money to make it work.

Figure 5

We closed our company down for a day and took every-body away to a local conference centre, where I and several people from Domino put on a joint presentation, which we called a Company-Wide Quality Improvement Awareness Day. This was quite an experience for some of my employees, many of them had not been in a classroom environment for some 40 years. However, I really wanted them to understand that this was a start of a journey and not just one of Ken Lewis' flavours of the month, for which I had previously been notorious.

To this day we still use the same programme for all new Dutton employees. In fact, we still work with Domino to bring new employees together and share the 'awareness experience' at Domino's premises at Bar Hill, Cambridge.

So, what were some of the messages that we wanted to get across? The first was the need for change, and also what the real 'cost of quality' meant. More significantly, we talked about the cost to the organisation of poor quality. We had a

36

mixture of individual and group exercises, and video presentations, which made it fast-moving, action-packed and interesting. We asked the questions 'What are we here for?' and 'Why have a Quality-Improvement Programme?'. We explained about the changing needs of our customers and their expectations, and about internal customers. We discussed the nature of the competition and that it did not now come from Fred in his shed two miles away from us, but rather from Europe and the Pacific Rim companies. We told them that we were going to train all our employees to be involved in the management of their areas.

All these were very revolutionary ideas, and of course the employees didn't believe a word of it. We also talked about quality issues and quality Minis, and how quality touched every area of the company. Finally, we discussed how quality improvement was the greatest potential source of profits. And, after a very enjoyable lunch, questions and answers, the issuing of baseball caps, we all came away really hyped up and ready to go.

One year later, nothing had changed!

'Terrorists'

How was it then that despite all the enthusiasm and the preparation, we seemed to have got almost nowhere? Part of it was because I was ill-prepared myself. I, personally, still had to learn the full implications of what this cultural change really meant. One most important lesson was that in my company (and doubtless in yours) I had a bunch of 'terrorists', mostly amongst the middle managers. Six years later, and with the benefit of hindsight, I am better able to understand just exactly how and why we came to find ourselves in this position.

Most of my management team had been promoted (as indeed perhaps I had been) more by virtue of their technical skills rather than because of their man management skills. The foreman, the supervisors and the managers had all worked very hard to reach their positions, and, naturally enough, they were not easily persuaded to hand down the baton of responsibility to their colleagues. After all, if they were to and it all went wrong, they thought that it would be they who would get the blame. Moreover, they could also see that devolving responsibilities downwards could leave them exposed and without a proper role.

Thus, at the heart of the problem was fear: both fear of change and fear of losing out. Some of the middle management, it is true, were empire builders, but they were dedicated Dutton people who spent most of their time supporting the company, fire fighting, and in trying to meet the needs of what most considered a highly unreasonable customer base.

The problem with these managers was their attitude and their reluctance to adopt new ways of thinking. Changing the attitudes of others is, in my experience, very difficult, particularly at management level. I have tended to find, with people from the shop floor, that with good leadership they will follow you anywhere. Unfortunately, this is rarely the case with managers, which brought about the rather hard-nosed expression at Dutton: 'If you can't change the man, change the man.'

The first casualty of the cultural change was our quality manager. This was a bit of a blow to me, because in fact I had been under the impression that it was precisely for him that I thought I was doing all this. However, he was from the old school, and he kept on reminding me that they had tried all this at his previous large international company 10 years earlier, and that it had never worked. He had his department, staffed by three inspectors, and he was not remotely interested in opening his mind to the possibility that his colleagues on the shop floor could actually produce zero-defect products without inspection. A heavy smoker, he left as a result of a newly-introduced No Smoking Policy, which I think he found was the thin end of the wedge.

His departure presented us with the opportunity to look at our inspection department, and here we came to the major conclusion that you cannot inspect quality into a product; it has to be built into a product.

Another factor that influenced our thinking was linked to the completion of their apprenticeships by two of our young staff members. There was I, after spending around £50,000 on each for years of technical and academic training, having to tell them that their work needed to be checked by someone else! The situation seemed absurd.

In our company, even then, whenever we wanted to effect a major step change, we would bring everybody together as early as possible to start discussions around the policy change. The question of what to do about the Inspection Department was so major that, once again, we got everyone together. I believe that this point in our company history marked both a watershed and also the first tangible empowerment that we gave our workforce.

After a number of meetings, we took the dramatic decision to abolish the Inspection Department. We redeployed our inspectors back as operatives on to the shop floor. All the doom-mongers warned about our reject rate soaring, both in-house and with goods being delivered to customers, and I confess to having been somewhat apprehensive myself. However, over the past six years, I can honestly say that we consistently hit zero defects to our customers month after month. Furthermore, I am equally convinced it would have been impossible to achieve that with inspectors in place.

Such results were not, of course, achieved in isolation; they stemmed from an amalgam of all the other changes that we made in our organisation and which will be covered in later chapters. But, no more do we hear the cry in our company of 'Inspection passed it!'. Everyone in the company has personal ownership of quality, and, moreover, we expect the same of our suppliers. This means that we do not need to have a goods-inwards inspection department either.

This was the first major step change in our organisation. When, in 1989, we launched our programme, we decided not to use the words Total Quality Management. It sounds too highfalutin' for us engineers. We adopted a simpler name; we called our programme 'The Dutton Way'.

So what precisely is 'The Dutton Way'? We describe it thus: *The Dutton Way is how to eliminate waste and fire fighting by working smart, not hard, and having fun at work.* In the presentations and lectures I give around the UK, I always ask the attendees how many of them are having fun at work. If my audiences are typical, I am sorry to say that very few of you are. However, if you go down the same route as us, in the same way that we have, I can assure you that you will end up having fun at work.

Goal-Setting

In 1989, we set ourselves a series of goals. These were as follows:

1. To simplify the manufacturing process.
2. To reduce working inventory.

3. To increase the skills flexibility of the workforce.
4. To maintain and improve product quality.
5. To be very customer-focused.

These are all wonderful motherhood statements; but what exactly did we have to do to achieve them?

1. Simplifying the manufacturing process

This came to mean that we would have to work much more closely with our customers' design departments, and to encourage them to design their products around our manufacturing processes. For this to occur, the first building block that had to be in place was a move to partnership sourcing, something that was a very new concept here in 1989.

What used to happen with us (and still does with many other companies) was that our customers would design their products without any reference to us as their suppliers. They would put the drawings and specifications to the purchasing department, who would then go out and get a minimum of three quotes for the manufacture of the components, generally taking the lowest price tendered. In my view, with any three organisations manufacturing similar products, each of them will tend to have a certain competitive edge in certain of their processes, not always in the technological field. Customers, though, rarely seem to design around these particular strengths. Thus (and this was the case with Dutton) they seldom get the real benefit of their suppliers' competitive advantage.

We began actively to encourage our customers' design departments to carry out relatively small changes to suit our capability, and, in doing so, considerable gains were made in terms of the final competitiveness of their products. For example, we persuaded them to use the nuts, studs, locks and hinges that we were buying, rather than going off into other new and somewhat obscure components that often could be difficult to obtain and expensive to assemble.

Of course, when one starts to go down the partnership sourcing route, a number of issues begin to emerge; and these can often be very worrying for customers. For instance, what in fact is the real role of the purchasing department going to be if you continue to have subcontractors working with designers?

On the other hand, it is just common sense to agree with the designers the selling price of the product before any actual development takes place, and this you can do all the better if the production engineer is looking to fit products around his own processes and strengths. With such simultaneous engineering, you can expect to get your products into the marketplace in a quarter of the time it used to take. Another advantage is that, since the majority of the creases will have already been ironed out, the changes required when you actually go into production are generally very few.

2. Reducing working inventories

This can only be achieved effectively if you build partnerships with the companies in your supply chain. We shall be talking about partnership sourcing later, but it is well worth saying now that it is a very effective way to reduce your overdraft.

Over the years, we always used to carry some £275,000 of work in progress and stock each month. Now, despite having increased our sales by 100 per cent, our stock and average work in progress at the end of each month has been as low as £27,000.

3. Increasing the skills flexibility of the workforce

In the past we used to employ apprentice-trained welders, sheet-metal workers, break-press operators, etc. Later chapters describe how we encouraged these people to multi-skill and to work in cross-functional teams.

4. Maintaining and improving product quality

Continuous improvement is really the cornerstone of Total Quality Management. In our company, the job specification is to do the job and to improve it. This meant that the company needed to have in place methods of collecting this data so that we could all identify the improved product quality and service.

5. Being very customer-focused

At the end of the day, we went out to discover what our customers really wanted and where they were going; and we sought to find out what part our company could play in helping them achieve their goals.

These were our goals, and to achieve them we had to bring about a fundamental change in the way we managed our business. Such a change also meant improving our customer image, our product quality, the competitive cost of our products, and the overall efficiency of our organisation.

Back in 1989, we had not the slightest idea of the pain that we would go through in trying to achieve everything we set out to do; but, as the saying goes: there is no gain without pain, and even in hindsight I would not change a single one of those goals or statements.

Becoming 'World Class'

In the early days (and it is still true today), we thought of what we were doing as a journey to excellence. Nowadays, perhaps we should call it a journey towards becoming a world-class manufacturing company. I think that the two things mean the same, and the Cranfield University definition of what constitutes a world-class manufacturer is certainly one that I would go along with.

Let's go through the Cranfield definition one point at a time.

1. *World-class manufacturing means top management commitment to manufacturing as a competitive weapon.* In my view, this means that the whole of the company should be committed to using the resources of the company to beat the competition. Often it is just the sales and marketing departments that are considered to be the competitive part of the company. This is just plain nonsense. Companies should be such that every employee takes on board the responsibility of the elimination of waste and of driving down costs.

2. *A strong customer focus.* We have changed from being just a reactive company to being highly proactive with our customers, seeking all the time to understand what they are trying to achieve. True, sometimes it can be extremely difficult to obtain this information, since many customers might not be as advanced or as progressive as you are. But if you spend enough time on this area you can really get down to what their ambitions are, and to where they think they are going. After all, as one of their suppliers, you will need to be part of that process.

3. *Awareness of best-practice techniques.* Dutton Engineering is privileged to be a host company for the

Department of Trade and Industry's *Inside UK Enterprise* scheme. The initiative gives all companies in the UK the opportunity to visit some 120 organisations that are perceived to be using best-practice techniques. This book features some of the best-practice techniques we have employed over the last six years, and, for those who are serious about changing for the better, it is most important to make time in your busy working week to get out and see best practice in operation for yourselves.

4. *Flexibility.* This is crucial in an uncertain and rapidly changing world. Things will never be the same as they were. Nowadays, customers want choice, at low prices; and we have to be able to provide accordingly or they will just go elsewhere. We have to be flexible and grab the opportunities before the competition does.

5. *Continuous product and Process innovation.* If you don't change you will always get the same results. So, we must always be out there seeking the latest products to enhance our customers' product performance and keep them buying from us. Process innovation must not be stifled by standards. Standards are there to be exceeded.

6. *World-class manufacturing is not a scatter-gun attempt to be best at everything.* In my company, we looked and decided what we were really good at. We then subcontracted out those things that we were not so good at. For instance, we used to have our own van, which ran around the country. We now have a single-sourced contractor who delivers all our goods over the UK and into Europe.

We also used to do our own gardening. This was subcontracted out to a landscape gardener, and we immediately won the Best-Kept Factories Premises award in Sandy. So really look at your own organisation: decide what you are really good at and subcontract out the rest – to good quality suppliers.

The Journey Onwards

So, now we are on our journey to excellence. We have passed one or two milestones, and we understand what is required of us to be a world-class organisation or manufacturing company. We are starting to focus on our external customers and their needs. Britain wants to welcome to its shores (Figure 6) all the nations of the world, to buy from us the goods and services we have to offer. This is how we can continue to enjoy, in the future, the kind of living standards we currently have.

Figure 6

But, as we have already seen, in our organisations there are 'terrorists' at all levels, people who are unable to grasp the nettle of change. The fact is that we all have to face up to these changes (no matter where we are in the organisation) and become champions of change. We have to drag

46

ourselves into the 21st century, because no one else can, or will, do it for us. We have to learn to improve both our internal and external systems.

For example, here I often use the words of Phil Crosby, one of the American gurus, who preached the philosophy of: 'Do it right the first time'. I usually ask the audience which word they think is the most important word. Most people plump for 'right', 'do' or 'first'. Very few come up with the answer I am looking – the word 'it'. How can you do *it* right the first time, if you do not know what *it* is?

For example, in Figure 7 the character on the left is trying to explain to his colleague what it is that he wants. Clearly he is failing in his task, because our friend on the right thinks he is talking about a stone wheel.

Such miscommunication was demonstrated to me in real life at one of the training seminars we were holding for all our employees. They were all involved in a group activity, identifying internal customers and finding ways of making their colleagues' jobs easier.

Figure 7

47

Next to our Accounts Executive sat one of our apprentices. In those days, we used to collect our workshop data on hand-written time sheets, on which each employee was meant to put down the work station and the time spent on one or other particular task. At the end of each week, the Accounts Department collated all this data, only to find that the information was often badly written, sometimes with figures transposed, all covered with coffee stains, and so on.

In the course of her discussion with the apprentice, our Accounts Executive soon realised that her young colleague did not understand just why he had to enter this information, nor what she did with it. Armed with this insight, the Accounts Executive called all the staff together and showed them exactly what she used the information for. This showed up the need for accuracy: to indicate whether or not jobs were making money, and to identify just how much time was disappearing down black holes in the company. It took just a single, half-hour session for her to explain the whole process.

Ever since then, the question of accuracy has become a non-issue. This is so much the case that we now collect all our data on computer, with the operators using bar coding and touch screens.

At Dutton, we, in management, have now learnt that it is our role to encourage all our colleagues to bring their brains and hearts to work with them instead of requiring them to hang them on the hooks in the cloakroom (Figure 8). If you find this unconvincing and believe that it is an impossible task, ask your staff what they do in the evenings after work or what they get up to in their spare time. I discovered, for example, that one of my polishers runs an amateur football team. That means getting the players together for practice match on cold, wet Wednesday evenings and arranging for

Figure 8

the transport, the football kit, the oranges, bottles of water and first aid all to arrive some 20-30 miles away on a Sunday morning. This is a complicated organisational activity. And yet he was not doing this at work. Why not? My view is because we, the management, generally put too many barriers in the way, and nobody expected it of him.

You will find among your own employees a great breadth of talent and skill. If you can channel this powerful force in the right direction, you will certainly have something truly dynamic on your side with which to face your competition.

4

Kaizen – Continuous Improvement

The Japanese word *Kaizen* is becoming increasingly familiar to those within the business environment, and, like so many words, it has a variety of different meanings. *Kaizen* can mean 'frog' (Figure 9), implying capable of small jumps, but it can also mean (and this is how we interpret it in the Western world) 'continuous improvement'.

Figure 9

51

Some years ago I read an article saying that on average, in Western companies, for every 100 employees in a company only 11 ideas are forthcoming from the workforce (Figure 10). In Japanese companies, the equivalent figure is 3,500 (Figure 11). With such a large variation in numbers it is clear that there is some fundamental difference in the way in which they operate their improvement schemes.

Figure 10

Figure 11

A Japanese colleague of mine told me that this in fact is Japan's greatest secret. As usual in life, it is the simple idea that is often the most effective, and in the case of *Kaizen* there is an additional bonus: the empowerment of your workforce, which gives them growing confidence to take the company forward.

In my experience there are two types of company (Figure 12). One tends to rely heavily on the big idea – major innovations and improvements. In such companies, the senior management are constantly seeking new ways to transform the company. The other type of company is a *Kaizen* company, one in which they also look for small, incremental improvements.

Figure 12

So, what do I mean by major innovations? I mean, for example, the introduction of a new machine tool, a new computer system, a new product, or perhaps a new managing director who is really going to shake things up. What tends to happen here, however, is that, having taken the giant innovative step, companies often then fall asleep again until the next step change is brought about (Figure 13). In my company things are different (Figure 14). We still have our step changes, but we also lay much emphasis on small improvements that require neither large sums nor much time or effort to achieve.

Figure 13

Figure 14

Most innovation needs the involvement of a large number of people to achieve the improvement. Even in my company, if a drawing needs to be changed many people are involved, and the time it takes to carry through the change can be quite considerable. But with our approach to *Kaizen* we focus on simple, small improvements which can be quickly carried out by the proposer.

Figure 15

In most companies or organisations at the present time, some 20 per cent of the people are actively involved in continuous improvement right now (Figure 15). It is a natural part of their daily lives. They are always looking for ways of making their job easier, safer and more productive. Unfortunately, most companies do not even know who these people are because there is no formal system in place to collect information about the improvements they carry out.

A further 60 per cent of employees tend to be quite happy to go on in same the old way. They have their job description; they know the times they should attend; they do the job to the specification required; the boss seems satisfied; and the customers appear content.

The remaining 20 per cent are what I tend to call the 'dinosaurs'. These are the people who are never, or almost never, going to change. For them, it is not their responsibility to improve either their own performance or that of the company. They have come to believe or accept that this is the management's responsibility. My suggestion is that you focus your efforts on trying to win over to *Kaizen* just the middle 60 per cent of those in your organisation. Succeed in that, and, given that you have already got the active 20 per cent, I think you will find the results startling.

At Dutton, it took us a full two years to get to the position where the last person in our company carried out a *Kaizen*. For him, and for 'dinosaurs' in general, doing a *Kaizen* is really quite an experience. In addition to the reward to one's own self-esteem of being able to receive recognition for that improvement, there is the added extra bonus of the personal fulfilment of becoming part of the whole company-wide team.

The University of Brighton's Centre for Business Research, in their extensive study on continuous improvement techniques, have identified three vehicles for continuous improvement: the truck, the medium-sized vehicle, and the bicycle (Figure 16).

The truck represents the large step changes that will be driven by the senior management team within organisations. Such step changes address major issues and require long timescales to produce results. The trucks represent the articulated lorries and supertankers of the continuous-improvement fleet. Then come the medium-sized vehicles – vans and cars – typically cross-functional teams of two to three people who are usually involved in specific projects running over a

Figure 16

few months. These might be corrective-action or process-improvement teams. For the Kaizen scheme I am advocating, the vehicles we need are bicycles.

Driving an articulated lorry safely requires considerable specialised training, and such vehicles are expensive to run and difficult to maintain. Even driving small cars and vans takes a considerable amount of skill and practice, and, here too, the costs are very significant. With bicycles, however, almost everybody can learn to ride them quickly, safely and with a minimum of training. Furthermore, given the right circumstances, they find the whole experience most enjoyable.

So the focus of *Kaizen* at Dutton is the bicycle. We encourage every employee to come up with at least one small incremental improvement that can be carried out immediately.

Western organisations tend to address their efforts towards big projects, the truck and light-van improvements. The problem here is that most people have not been trained to be able to make any worthwhile contribution to such improvements. In some cases, it is true, they are not capable of putting in anything, but mostly they are not even asked to contribute.

Up until now, management has tended to ignore the bicycle. We have found that if we target our efforts on the bicycles and encourage people to develop their skills and ability to carry out small improvements, the light vans and trucks develop naturally, and with much more effectiveness.

Suggestion Schemes

In the West, most people's experience of participating in the running of their company is the traditional suggestion scheme. Here, suggestion boxes are more or less liberally scattered around the place; the suggestions are generally reviewed once a month by a senior management team, and the value of any award is generally a reflection of its value in terms of the cost savings to the company.

There are many disadvantages with these schemes: the implementation process can be lengthy; often the senior management do not fully understand the real implications of the suggestion, and generally they have little or no knowledge of the person putting forward the idea. Frequently, the worst scenario happens: the suggestion is placed in the box and then disappears never to be heard of ever again. This is hardly a situation calculated to encourage a free flow of constructive suggestions. If you want a thriving, ideas-laden company, the traditional suggestion scheme needs to go!

Part of the process of developing a *Kaizen* company involves breaking down the complacency of the middle 60 per cent of company staff mentioned above (those who feel

Figure 17

comfortable in their warm bath) (Figure 17). My recommendation is that you paint reality as it is, with a view to getting them to grasp the fact that the competition are after you (and them) (Figure 18), placing logs on your fire and turning you all into boiled frogs before you know it. To launch this scheme, you should get together all your employees and arrange for a presentation to be given by the most senior person in the organisation. This will show real commitment from the top.

Figure 18

The following is some of the material I used in my own presentation to illustrate the level of improvements we were looking for. As a great fan of fairground bumper cars, I chose such an operation as an example.

The Bumper Car Example

Many of you, I am sure, have been to the fairground when travelling fairs have visited your town or village. And, perhaps, some of you have been to the large theme parks which have been developing across the country. Well, one of the rides I always enjoy is the bumper cars. These always give me a great opportunity to crash into everyone, perfectly legally, and to spin around to the sound of blaring music.

But, if you think about it, these cars have to be well looked after by the men who collect the money, and, especially, by the mechanics who keep them in a safe working condition. In this imaginary scenario, I want you to focus on one of their recurrent problems: frequently the staff come across nuts that have fallen off one or other of the bumper cars (Figure 19).

On each occasion when these nuts are discovered on the rink, the find is reported to the manager. He in turn reports the problem back to the distributor; the distributor in turn reports back to the manufacturers of the bumper car, and so the process goes on. Well, this all obviously takes masses of time and effort, and consequently the manufacturer has to find design and development time to address the problem of the nuts coming off the existing models they are selling. The process might take months or years for the design to be changed to new models and eventually to put right in the field those cars that they have already sold. However, none

Figure 19

of this of course helps our mechanics, who are facing the problem on a day-to-day basis.

So, to tackle the problem, what might the *Kaizen* mechanics do? The first thing the mechanics do is discuss the problem with their manager or team leader. The first difficulty is that the surface of the rink is black with lots of skid marks, which makes it very difficult to find the nuts. Knowing that there was always a good chance that nuts would have fallen of in the course of a day, the conscientious mechanics would often stay back until late at night to try to find them (Figure 20).

This was time-consuming – and highly frustrating. Then, one mechanic came up with a bright idea which won his team leader's support. The idea was to paint all the nuts on all the cars white, so that when a nut fell off it would be easily seen. This was a *Kaizen*. Everyone was now able to spot the nuts quickly and remove them from the rink.

However, this shed light on another problem: how to identify which car the nuts had fallen off. This was an

Figure 20

onerous and unpleasant task. Each car had to be turned on its side and inspected. A second *Kaizen* developed naturally out of the first. Since each car was a different colour, the next idea was to paint all the nuts the same colour as the car they were on (Figure 21). This meant that the mechanics could all locate any fallen nut easily on the rink and would have to turn over only one car to put the nut back on.

So what had the mechanic achieved? He had been able to make his work and that of his colleagues much easier, and he had improved the safety of the equipment they had to look after. Eventually modifications to solve the problem would come through; but in the meantime the mechanics had contributed to their operations by keeping their bumper cars operating for longer periods and making their own jobs easier and more enjoyable.

Before making a short presentation on similar lines to the staff in your organisation in order to help them understand the level and size of the improvements you are looking for, I think it is extremely important for you (or the most senior

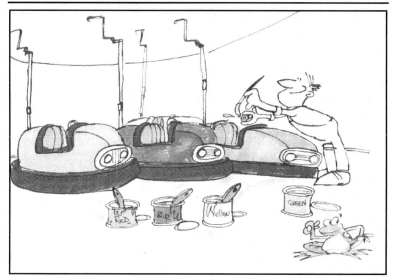

Figure 21

manager) to look around your own area and photograph a small improvement that you can tackle yourself. Here I emphasise small – nothing too grandiose or impressive. This would tend to intimidate the middle 60 per cent, who might not be drawn in because they might feel insufficiently confident to live up to your expectations. The audience needs to be able to relate the improvement so as to understand clearly what you are trying to achieve. Then let them get on with it and give as much encouragement as you can.

Team Leaders

Team leaders have a vital role to play in introducing and consolidating a *Kaizen* scheme of this kind, and it is here that the fundamental difference now starts to emerge between traditional suggestion schemes and *Kaizen* schemes. Senior management should have no role to play in the *Kaizen* scheme other than providing inspiration, coaching and support. This they should do by encouraging middle management to assist the team leaders in implementing the *Kaizen* scheme.

Naturally, this will involve some initial commitment of time. For the first few months after your initial presentation, you will have to spend some time with your team leaders, for whom all this will be very new, to ensure that they are really leading their teams and actually encouraging team members to come forward with *Kaizen* improvements. This often poses a challenge for supervisors, who, having probably risen to their position through their technical skills, might find it difficult to let go of some of their responsibility. It might also mean that you have to face some rather unpleasant truths: that not all your team leaders or supervisors are the best people for the job.

Your task as a senior executive is to ensure that your team leaders support *Kaizen* as enthusiastically as you do yourself. Given time, as the improvements start to come through, they will see that their own daily tasks become easier and they will have less problem-solving to do as their colleagues solve their own problems.

Figure 22 illustrates the only paperwork we use to record and monitor our *Kaizens*. We deliberately kept our *Kaizen* form as simple as possible. The last thing an enthusiastic employee wants is a complicated document to do battle with. It is important to remember that many people, especially at the grass-roots level of the organisation, do not handle paperwork on a day-to-day basis. This can result in their having an in-built dread of form-filling. Team leaders are usually aware of team members who lack confidence in expressing themselves in writing, and it would be appropriate for them to help their colleagues with this burden.

Dutton Engineering (Woodside) Ltd

KAIZEN

Date: ....

Name: ....

Team Leader: ....

Title:

Please describe your Kaizen briefly with illustration on back of this form:

Before Improvement (Problem)	After Improvement (Kaizen)

Effect

Evaluation

Award £

Group Leader ...... Managing Director ...... Accounts ......
(initials)

Figure 22

At Dutton, our team leaders hold the *Kaizen* forms and, when one of the team members comes up with an improvement, he or she discusses it initially with the team leader. It is they who discuss the feasibility or viability of carrying out the *Kaizen*. The form is then completed with the person's name, the team leader's name, the date and title of the proposal, the initial problem and the after-improvement effect. The improvement is then evaluated, and here, in my view, the evaluation process should go much wider than just an assessment of the financial benefits. Many of the *Kaizens* might not initially appear to save the company any money, but once implemented they might introduce a whole raft of benefits. A *Kaizen* that does no more than to make people feel happier is still of great benefit, particularly as it will endow the *Kaizen* scheme with that magical and somewhat illusive feel-good factor.

Our team leaders also have the role of checking with their colleagues from other teams to see whether a similar idea has been put forward. Having ascertained that the idea is something new, the team leader encourages the proposer to go off and gather the necessary resources for carrying out the improvement. The back of the *Kaizen* form is used for any diagrams or sketches required to assist in understanding the proposal for improvement.

When the improvement has been implemented, the team leader passes the signed *Kaizen* form to the managing director. I think that it is vitally important that the MD or most senior person in the company looks at the *Kaizen* initially to reinforce commitment from the top. Employees gain a lot of satisfaction from receiving recognition for their efforts. All too often employees only come to the attention of senior management when there are problems, and this is especially true in large organisations. Front-line employees can come to feel so far removed from the top echelons of the company that they deem they have no significant part (if any at all) to play in the running of the company. We all respond well to a pat on the back and that wonderful feeling of a job well done.

Having signed the *Kaizen* form to indicate that he has seen it, the managing director should then pass it straight away to Accounts for immediate payment of the award money. Many visitors to my company have been shocked at the small amount of money that we award for each *Kaizen*. However, there is method in this apparent meanness. Such awards are neither divisive nor do they constitute a drain on resources. It makes tangible the employees' contribution while emphasising the process and not the result.

At Dutton, the team leaders are those who decide the level of the award: either £5 or £15. As of 1 April 1994, such awards may be awarded free of tax and National Insurance, fitting, as they do, within the Inland Revenue criteria of awards up to £25. The team leader's assessment of the value of the award should not always, in my view, be related to the amount of money that might be saved by the company each year by the improvement, but rather in terms of the overall value to the proposer of the idea. This is because one *Kaizen* often leads on to two, three or four further improvements. Moreover, some improvements have financial benefits downstream, particularly where green issues are concerned.

Equally, it could be that the team leader might wish to give a £15 award to someone who has never done a *Kaizen* before as an encouragement to continue going down this route. The level of the award might be based on the degree of initiative shown by the proposer, or on the effort that was made outside working hours to achieve the *Kaizen*.

At the beginning of this initiative I myself fell into the old trap. I could not resist the old management practice of putting controls into the system, particularly where money is concerned. I said to the team leaders that only one in four awards could be worth £15, the rest being worth £5 (Figure 23).

Figure 23

What later transpired, and what staggered me, was the degree of care all my staff, especially the team leaders, exercise when dealing with the company's money and resources. I was, in fact, forced to intervene when, as the *Kaizens* started coming through, I found that they were mostly £5 awards. Many is the time I have had to ask team leaders to increase the figure to £15 (Figure 24).

Figure 24

So, how do we actually motivate everyone in the company to do a *Kaizen*, particularly the 20 per cent of 'dinosaurs'? Here again we rely on the training of the team leaders. After all, it is their job is to encourage everyone in the team to do a *Kaizen*. Some of the most successful improvements have been where a team leader has sown the seed of a suggestion to someone who had never before put forward a *Kaizen*. You would be surprised at the effect of letting people mull over an idea in their minds. Often, this process can result in people returning the next day with their first improvement. In your company some people might never have done (or been asked to do) anything creative in their working lives before – such was the case at Dutton. In these circumstances, the introduction by the individuals themselves of their *Kaizens* can often be highly enjoyable and fulfilling.

In training team leaders and tasking them to get everyone in their team to complete a *Kaizen*, I have often used the example of Gladys (Figure 25), who had worked previously in

Figure 25

the test section of an electronics company for over 10 years. At Dutton, part of her job was to put four plugs on the back of the test equipment, take a reading, and then pull off each individual plug. Gladys had never completed a *Kaizen* before, so her team leader made her a wooden puller, which made it easier for her to pull off two plugs at a time (Figure 26).

Figure 26   *Figure 27*

That night, Gladys went home and told her husband, Fred, all about the wooden puller that her team leader had made for her. Fred, a great DIY fanatic, discussed Gladys' job with her, and the next day in walked Gladys, pleased as Punch, with an even larger wooden tool edged with some rubber to protect the test equipment from damage. She could now use both hands and pull off four plugs at once (Figure 27). Having been able to carry out this first improvement was a great incentive for Gladys, and she now had sufficient confidence to look at other areas of her job that could be improved.

Top management's leadership and commitment to the process can best be shown if they do the first *Kaizen*. My first one took in a long-standing problem. For some 10 years I used to come to work each day through a particular door in the corridor leading into my office area. Every morning, I would kick a wooden wedge under the door to keep it open. Since we have a wooden floor, the vibrations caused by people coming up the stairs would often cause the wedge to move, resulting in the door closing – invariably as I was walking towards it with a cup of coffee in one hand and a pile of papers in the other.

My *Kaizen* was to go to the local hardware store and buy a hook and eye, get hold of an electric drill from the maintenance department and fit the hook and eye myself on a Saturday morning. This example reinforced to everyone in the company the type of improvements I was looking for. And, of course, almost every one in the company recognised that such a simple task was well within their own capabilities.

The very first *Kaizen* that came from the shop floor after the launch of our award scheme involved our scrap bin. For 10 years the bin had been located in one of the slots in the car park. The suggestion was that the bin be moved so that it would not be the first thing visitors saw when arriving at the factory. The bin was moved onto the left-hand side of the path on some spare ground, and in the process (and this the operator had not foreseen) created another car parking space worth perhaps £250 a year to the company. This is often the case with *Kaizen:* the original idea can result in many other benefits that are not always apparent at the time.

Kaizens should come from every part of the company, including the administrative side of the business or organisation. Isobel, then our secretary, devised a *Kaizen* that tackled our order processing system and saved considerable amounts of time and money. Our order forms used to have blue, pink, yellow and white copies. One would be sent to the supplier, and the others filed in various parts of the company. It was all very expensive and time-consuming. Isobel's idea was to print the order on headed paper and retain all the information in the computer. Simple, but it enabled us to get rid of all the other bits of paper and the storage necessary for them.

Two other administrative *Kaizens* are worth mentioning here. At Dutton, our reception area is unmanned and when visitors arrive they have to pick up the phone and state their business to the telephone operator. Since we operate partnership sourcing and have long-term agreements with all our suppliers, we are very choosy about seeing representatives from other companies, and then only by appointment. Having to tell the same story politely to representative after representative used to take up a considerable amount of time. However, from the representatives' point of view, since they were sometimes tasked to approach every company on our industrial estate, they would need to come away with a company brochure or compliments slip as proof of their visit.

Isobel's first *Kaizen* was to leave brochures and compliments slips on the table in the reception area, thereby saving her many unnecessary trips. However, after this *Kaizen* was implemented, it was often found that the visitors would leave our brochures and compliments slips in an untidy state. The second *Kaizen* was to put up a letter rack. End of problem.

These changes may appear small, but they set the tone in our company and led on to major discoveries. One of these was that *Kaizen* made us completely reassess our investment programme. In engineering companies the cry tends to be that to increase the company's profitability and improve business performance, one must have very latest machine tools, capable of being set up quickly and having ever-faster production speeds. Over the years at Dutton, we have found that by using *Kaizen* improvements this strategy has not been necessary for us to achieve our goals. This is because it often happens that neither equipment suppliers nor buyers understand the full capabilities of the tools they have sold or bought. Only those who work with the tools really know what their machines are fully capable of. The fact is that we did not buy a major new machine tool for over five years; we did not need to. Over time we discovered that the tools are far more versatile than we ever thought possible.*

A good example of what I mean is our Grainmaster machine. With this, the operator feeds through pieces of material that are grained and carried by a conveyor to the rear of the machine. Since the machine is very large, the operator is unable to see what is happening behind the machine. This used to mean that we needed two people to operate it: one to load and one to clear the grained metal. The *Kaizen* in this case was to put a mirror on top of the machine, so the operator at the front could now see what was going on at the rear of the machine. Naturally, of course, as sheet metal workers we did not waste money buying a mirror; we just polished up a piece of scrap stainless steel, which did the trick. This small *Kaizen* has shown, and continues to show, substantial cost savings.

Another series of *Kaizens* were brought in by Helen, now retired, who worked with us for three years assembling the ink-jet printers we manufacture. Before she joined Dutton, Helen had never worked in engineering; in fact, she had spent the previous ten years running a pub with her husband.

Helen's first Kaizen was to relocate a roll of paper to just underneath her desk. For years, the paper had been located at the other side of the factory and each day Helen used to have to go to the roll and collect armfuls of paper so that she could do her day's work without having to trudge over to the roll location.

Her second *Kaizen* was to have the racks of screws, nuts, bolts, washers and hinges relocated from the far side of her bench to the right-hand side of her bench. This reduced the

---

In 1997, we undertook a considerable re-tooling investment plan to gear up for the growth in business resulting from the increased demand for our services.

stretching she had to do to get hold of the components she required.

Her third *Kaizen* was the purchase of a small lift truck so that she could lift the by-now heavy printers on her own onto the stillages before packaging ready for despatch. The truck cost £450 at that time, which in fact was the most expensive item we ever bought for any of the *Kaizens* that were carried out. Helen now had a piece of equipment she could adjust to the right working height, and she no longer needed anyone else's help to load the completed assemblies onto the stillages.

Her fourth *Kaizen* was to have a turntable built on top of the lift truck to avoid walking around the cabinet during the assembly process. Here was someone without any previous engineering experience fully capable of carrying out quite sophisticated production engineering because of her experience of doing her job. All these improvements made her job easier, safer and more enjoyable.

I mentioned earlier that 20 per cent of the people in any company are already carrying out small improvements, and that this is a very natural thing for them to do. However, unless you have system in place to collect the necessary data you are unlikely to know who these people are.

One member of our staff, Jack, our *Kaizen* champion, came to us having worked for two large companies, each for some 15-20 years. He was made redundant by both. Clearly, not having systems indicating what the 'Jacks of this world' were doing for them, neither of these companies had the remotest idea of what Jack had been up to. Jack is a natural at continuous improvement. He is very orderly and likes things kept tidy. Among his *Kaizens* are a wooden structure he made at home to dispense with our quality control batch tickets; a laminated assembly-instruction display; a tool board showing the 'home' of the various tools for those other

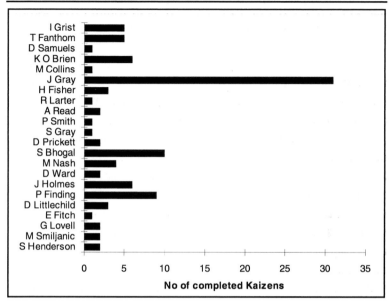

Figure 28

members of the multi-functional teams that use this bench at various times, and so on. In fact, after the first 100 *Kaizens* had been carried out and we decided to see who had been the most proactive person, we found out that, of the 100, Jack Gray had carried out 32.

You are, I would suggest, currently employing many Jack Grays – people who do not just sit there and continue to do the same thing in the same way. They will continue to make things easier for themselves and others, even if it is only by moving a filing cabinet from one position to another. With our system the Jack Grays of this world can be identified and rewarded for their skills and talents in improving the performance of the company.

With the first 100 *Kaizens*, we also wanted to see the areas that the improvements had affected. Of these, 12.4 per cent were to do with communications. The ideas included the introduction of wipe boards around the company for leaving messages; improving the paperwork systems and cutting out our once previously huge requirements for paperwork storage. In the process, we discovered that most of the reasons for which we had kept the paperwork were no longer relevant to our operation.

Another 33 per cent of the *Kaizens* were linked to specific product improvements. Now that we work much closer with our customers on design, where often 80 per cent of the costs get locked in, there is still a remaining 20 per cent of cost that represent improvement opportunities for those actually doing the work. It is in such areas that we can really delight our customers by giving them price reductions brought about by sharing with them the cost reductions we have been able to achieve.

Our results have shown a 25 per cent improvement in terms of the performance of our machine tools and equipment, and 20 per cent in terms of environmental improvements. One of these concerned the aluminium cans from our soft drinks vending machine. These are now collected together and recycled in a proper manner. Last, but not least, 9.7 per cent of the *Kaizens* were produced by the administrative people in the company (Figure 29).

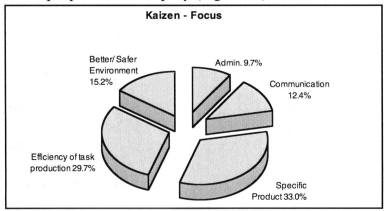

Figure 29

Now we come to the bit that the accountants like. What did it cost us to do these *Kaizens*, and how much waste did we drive out of our business? Figure 30 tells it all. We spent £750 in awards of £5 and £15 for each *Kaizen*; £1,670 for labour, material and equipment to do the *Kaizens* – a total investment of just over £2,400. The result: we drove £160,000 of waste out of Dutton!

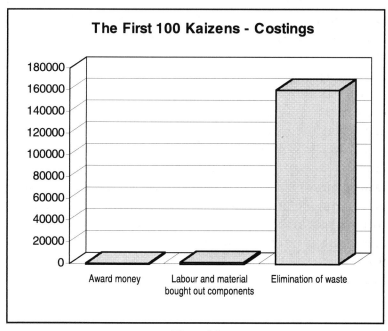

Figure 30

A similar level of waste is waiting to be driven out of your organisation. What is more, it is very easy at the beginning, because this kind of waste is hanging well within the reach of everyone within your organisation. But the process does not end there. A *Kaizen* award scheme continues to engender major benefits as the years go by. First, if your competitors are not involved with continuous improvement in the same way, you should soon start to gain a competitive edge on them. Your people will soon begin to have an impact on their own day-to-day working environment. Your workforce will start to feel empowered to cause change to happen within your organisation, and will really have a sense of ownership. People who may never previously have done anything creative at work will start to gain a feel-good factor that will spread to permeate throughout the company. Their confidence in tackling areas of waste and problem-solving will grow by leaps and bounds.

Personally, I was astonished at the level and scope of the improvements we were able to achieve. This process will keep a total quality management initiative ball rolling along, and often develops a sense of friendly rivalry among departments to see who can come up with the most original or greatest number of improvements. *Kaizen* liberates employees, and they begin to feel able to participate fully. Tasks and activities that have been performed in the same way for years cease to remain sacrosanct as the perception is changed that the way things are is the way management wants them to be.

Kaizen shows that they can make good quality decisions for themselves and provides them with an opportunity to use their individual talents and expertise for everyone's benefit. Interestingly enough, after a few years, and the initial upsurge of creativity, we have discovered that people start to regard continuous improvement as a natural part of their daily life and do *Kaizens* without putting them in as official changes.

That is what your company will need to achieve in order to remain at the leading edge. To improve the performance of the company you must use the talents and creativity of your workforce to the full (Figure 31).

Kaizen

Low in capital intensity, it depends for its success not on expensive machinery and equipment but on harnessing the creativity and enthusiasm latent in all employees of the organisation.

Figure 31

Continuous improvement is one of the greatest sources of profitability and success. Your people will stop asking 'Why doesn't the management...?' and start asking 'Why don't I just...?'. Later, this evolves naturally into 'Why don't we...?', and from this you will find multi-functional teams coming together to solve problems and tackle new projects.

5

The Way Forward
1 – Partnership Sourcing

Partnership sourcing – *a commitment by both customers and suppliers, regardless of size, to a long-term relationship based on clear, mutually agreed objectives to strive for world-class capability and competitiveness* – has been around for a good many years. Some areas of the automobile industry, for example, have been operating it since the early 1980s, but unfortunately it has been very slow to catch on with the rest of British industry. True, it can be very hard to move from the established way of doing things (purchasing on basis of the invoice price) to the more sensible, new way of purchasing (on the basis of the total cost of the acquisition of the products and services), but the benefits are clear. First, you know what the products or services really cost, and, second, you can then focus your activities on specific areas with a view to eradicating waste and getting your costs down.

All this, however, requires systems of measurement, and few companies and organisations are willing or able to set up the correct monitoring systems. They therefore continue to plough on in their old sweet way, usually at the behest of the Chief Executive, believing, or electing to believe, that the price they are paying on their invoice is, and should be, the main supply criterion. Where such an approach prevails – and, sadly, this is almost everywhere in the UK – suppliers tend to be seen as a constraining source causing lots of problems and having very little to add to the party.

At Dutton, we see the relationship with our suppliers somewhat differently. We consider our suppliers to be a valuable resource, with specialist knowledge, skills and equipment, which, if properly focused, will help improve our company's competitive performance. Our view is that our suppliers, as an integral part of our supply chain, must by definition play an integral part in our success. All chains are only as strong as their weakest link, and the same goes for supply chains. Unless you, your suppliers and your customers are all pulling in the same direction, none of you will ever succeed in turning in a world-class performance.

The definition of partnership sourcing cited above is a wonderful motherhood statement, pointing out, in my view, in a handful of words the way forward to achieving your goals and objectives. Many representatives who visit or telephone our company still find it difficult to understand what we mean by long-term relationships. They often ask if they can tender when we review our present arrangements, and seem to expect this to be every 12 months. This is not what we mean by a long-term relationship. We mean that our relationships are on-going and are based on quality performance backed by confidence and trust.

Our confidence exists because we maintain very close links with the companies in our supply chain. For example, our suppliers each have an electronic pass allowing them free access to any part of our company during our normal business hours. This means that, as they fill our *Kanban* bins, often on a daily basis, they can, and do, meet our management and team members as they wish to. It also allows us to meet them and maintain links, while at the same time providing an early warning signal, should one be needed, of any deterioration in their performance.

Once a year we have a Suppliers' Day, when we take all our suppliers out to lunch, explain what we have been up to in the previous year and outline our strategy for the next three years. By knowing where we are going, our suppliers are able then to plan confidently their own investments to meet our future needs. Each year we award our most outstanding supplier a 'Supplier of the Year' trophy, which suppliers go all out to win. This helps build up the rapport that is so essential for a strong and effective supply chain.

The key objectives of partnership sourcing are:

- *Minimising total costs.* As mentioned above, in reality invoice prices do not indicate the full cost of getting goods or services to where they are required in your organisation. When company executives believe that their purchasing departments have successfully completed their task if they have negotiated the lowest available price, they are neglecting whole areas of additional costs. What about rejects, rework and the other areas of the company affected by poor supplier performance? These should also be brought into the cost equation.

- *Maximising product and service development.* We, along with many other companies, have found that by working together with our customers we have been able to reduce significantly the time to market of our (and hence their) products. In addition, with fewer changes required, as production levels ramp up, a noticeable competitive advantage has been gained.

- *Obtaining competitive advantage.* At Dutton, we have found that joint activities between us and our suppliers has helped us to keep prices down and stable for four years – and this despite the world-wide increase in raw materials!

However, to get to this position requires very considerable trust, which can take many years to develop. In my view, when approaching the issue of partnerships the lead should always come from the customers. Our experience has shown that our suppliers have been much more willing to participate in partnering than many of our customers. Customers tend to be very sceptical about the free flow of information that is required. All this is perhaps understandable, because it changes the status of the 'expendable' supplier into a fully-fledged contributor to the overall productive process. Once customers have had a taste of the opportunities and benefits of the new relationship, however, they slowly start to inch their way down the road to closer relations with ever-increasing confidence.

As always in business, for new paths to be successfully explored the determining factor is genuine commitment from top-level management (Figure 32). Half-hearted and anodyne statements will not achieve anything. Building trust is neither a smooth process nor a quick fix. It really needs time, perhaps even years, to establish itself firmly. After all, it might involve throwing over perhaps a lifetime of alternative practices.

One major requisite for developing openness and trust, for example, involves open-book accounting, in which companies exchange accounts. The first time we did this our

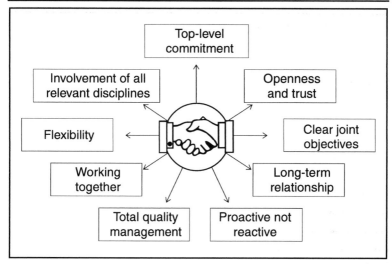

Figure 32

suppliers were completely dumbfounded. They had never previously received a set of accounts from any of their customers. Such an action indicates to the suppliers that what they are about to receive really is going to be different. It clearly displays your confidence in them as partners.

You will also need to set clearly understood, joint, long-term objectives, and agree which lines of communication are to be used. At Dutton, over the years, we have adhered strictly to the long-term nature of these partnerships, only changing suppliers when they have proved incapable of making the quantum leap forward that both we and partnership sourcing required.

As the years have gone by, however, things have not stood still; and, in the same way as our customers' demands have grown, so have ours, regarding suppliers' performance. Some of our suppliers have not lived up to their promise. One company that won our Supplier of the Year Award in the first year is no longer with us. Unfortunately, they were unable to bring themselves into line with the same performance standards as the rest of the companies in our supply chain.

Such relationships need to be highly proactive, as opposed to being merely reactive. We are not experts in banking, insurance, vehicle maintenance, or many of the other spheres required to keep an engineering company functioning effectively. Therefore, we look to our suppliers, as the specialists, and expect them to bring along with them the latest technology, equipment and techniques in their industry, so that we can integrate all this top-notch expertise into our supply chain and pass on the benefits accrued. For us to succeed, it is vitally important for our suppliers to have their own top-quality management who have a sense of vision and are sincere.

Another equally vital aspect for partnerships to be effective is that all departments of the various companies must work together, with all barriers broken down and all preconceived ideas shed. Attitudes in each of the companies must be flexible and sympathetic. There must be a strong will to win. The defending of empires, which is so common in industry, and its replacement by such departmental cooperation may involve some difficult decisions and may take a long time to achieve; but the old-style methods of purchasing (whereby both the buyer and the salesman each try to concede as little as possible) is definitely steadily on its way out as far as the best and most highly respected companies are concerned.

Today, purchasing needs to be a team effort, and this realisation might come to help soften some of the hard-bitten attitudes held by so many for so long.

Advantages for Purchasers

So, what are the advantages for purchasers in going down this route?

Security of supply

Partnerships should help ensure your company security of supply. No longer should it happen that your turn comes after that of more powerful purchasers. Also, your needs should soon come to be understood along the whole length of your supply chain.

But how do you get to this position and what steps need to be taken? Since you already have a supply chain, it is highly likely that you know who the good and bad suppliers are currently. I would recommend, if you have not already begun to do this, that you start to drop your poor suppliers and start developing your good ones. As your level of business increases with these good suppliers, you will generally start to become a more valued customer. You can then work towards the situation in which, when they deliver their products to you, if the first one is right then the last one will be right, too.

You should also seek to understand what your suppliers' plans are when faced by a disaster scenario. I am constantly amazed how often this information is not sought out by even the largest UK companies, despite the fact that they often do not carry stock themselves to cover such eventualities.

Partnership sourcing should also bring you on-time deliveries, because the supplier can now plan longer-term to meet your requirements, knowing that renegotiation will not get in the way. He will often be able to buy at better prices from his own sources of supply, and this should also be reflected both in the price and in his delivery performance. The quality of the products being supplied should steadily improve, as your suppliers are now confidently assured of your business. You should also find that they will begin investing in the right tools and equipment to satisfy your quality needs.

In our company, we have taken a policy decision to single source, i.e. to use just one supplier for particular product lines. This has added even greater advantages, particularly in terms of the amount of administrative controls we require to manage the process. Such a small basket of suppliers has meant that we could reduce the controls to an absolute minimum.

In our experience, once all-round confidence has been achieved and suppliers really understand (perhaps for the first time ever) where you are going and their place in this process, you will see them exceeding all your expectations.

Reduced paperwork

One of our trading conditions is that our suppliers are only allowed to send in one invoice each month. Since they are only going to get one payment per month, why do we need all those individual invoices flooding in? We receive a one-sheet summary, and they receive one payment. Actually, we have now taken this even further now. The monthly invoice now comes in on computer disk, coded according to our cost centres, which are entered by the supplier.

Each supplier has only one purchase order, which he retains forever. The supplier of our admin. materials, for example, has an order that states 'To supply material for the administrative functions as required'. Only once did a supplier try to pull a fast one. Our system of controls picked it up immediately. This broke the previous relationship of trust and we found an alternative source of supply.

Working closely with your suppliers, as the specialists in their own field, you should also see a reduction in your time to market performance, as well as a substantial reduction in the stocks you need to hold and a reduction in your total cost of acquisitions.

Simpler delivery systems

At Dutton, some 90 per cent of raw materials and consumables are now delivered using a *Kanban* system. This is a very simple and effective supply technique, generally based on a two-box system with one week's supply of components held in each box. When the first box is emptied, the operator places in a central position on the component rack a component-specific ticket detailing the component part number, description and quantity. The team operator then starts using the second week's box of components. In the meantime, the empty box with the ticket is collected by the supplier and refilled with one week's supply of components. The replenished box is replaced on the supplier's next visit, and the next set of tickets and empty boxes is collected.

In the four to five years that we have been operating this *Kanban* system, we have never yet run out of a component.

It is up to our suppliers to decide what batch sizes they can most efficiently manufacture, or buy in and buffer stock for us. This simple system has saved us all unimaginable amounts of time. A Dutton operator assembling an enclosure can confidently put out his hand, time after time, every time, to pick up nuts, bolts, hinges, locks, etc., all the while knowing that there will be a quality product there waiting for him. And all this without a special purchase order, or a

Goods Received or Inspection Department, etc. Nor do we need to make a telephone call, send a fax, or do anything else to get that product there. It is where it should be when we want it, with the minimum of administrative control.

Improved quality and cost savings

The entry point for anyone wishing to be a world-class manufacturer is quality products and service quality. Our experience of partnership sourcing has shown that our suppliers have both sharpened their standards and continually improved their performance quality. This has meant that our products and service levels have also improved, and we have been able to pass on the cost savings to our customers. By eliminating the goods-inwards inspection, for example, we made major cost savings, and it has become clear that if you share the right kind of quality culture with your suppliers many such costly and unnecessary expenses can be saved.

Faster product development

If you, the purchaser, can tap into the skills and strengths of your suppliers, you will be able to get into the marketplace a lot quicker with your products. Enormous competitive advantage can be achieved when your designers, drawing offices and purchasing departments are all working closely with your suppliers.

Lower stocks and smaller overdrafts

Lower stocks are another feature of partnerships, particularly if you adopt a *Kanban* system. Many companies should be

90

looking at a minimum of 25 stock turns per year, and could aim to set their sights at 50. With such reduced stock and reduced work in progress, your overdraft should shrink dramatically.

Reduced total cost

With the old-style adversarial relations, costs are often kept high because of the perpetual telephoning, contacting, cajoling, pushing and shoving that is necessary to remedy supply problems. Under these circumstances Murphy's law seems always to prevail, and the cost of rectifying the problems is always very high. The truth is, however, that very few companies actually measure their remedial, cost-of-quality expenditure, most of which is built in through outmoded and outdated systems of control.

With developed partnerships, by working together to introduce new-style collaborative systems, you should find the cost of running your business falling considerably and continuing to decline.

Advantages for Suppliers

Partnerships, by definition, are not there just for the customers. Suppliers, too, must see a range of significant benefits if they are to play ball.

Forward planning

For your suppliers, having long-term agreements will boost their confidence in terms of their ability to plan their own businesses.

Where long-term agreements are in place, your suppliers will be able, perhaps for the first time ever, to study your company's requirements and make their own forward plans regarding acquisitions of plant, equipment, premises and other developments that will enhance your business.

My view is that in the UK in the past (and for many companies this is still the case) we never really gave our suppliers the opportunity to perform to the best of their ability. Here, and in much of the West, we are much more used to the old supply methods and to short-termism. We are used to denying suppliers access to our design and development people, and yet it is precisely these people who generally appreciate the valuable input that suppliers can give. This has tended to act against product quality and has helped build in costs.

Over time, partnerships push suppliers into performing to their best ability, and often bring the suppliers renewed vigour and an enhanced sense of satisfaction. 'Win/win' moves from mere verbiage into reality. There is, moreover, another major upside. Such relationships encourage innovation and development, because suppliers no longer tend to feel that they are only being paid for what the customer has specified. They often start to look ahead to see what they can do to improve the customer's product.

Financial stability and payment on time

Partnerships depend on trust, and there can be no real partnership unless customers guarantee to pay their suppliers on time. There should also be plenty of scope for mutually beneficial financial arrangements, resulting in better cash flows and the effective pooling of resources.

Virtually all companies experience cash flow problems at some time or other; but where regular payments have become the norm in your supply chain much more help and support tends to be provided by both your customers and suppliers. After all, it is in everyone's interest that such temporary setbacks are resolved.

Reduced total costs

Suppliers can enjoy the benefit of seeing reduced total costs if they themselves adopt the somewhat radical ideas put forward here. Figure 33 shows the steamship of cost sailing along captained by a traditional purchasing department that focuses on price. To be fair to the crew, this is probably exactly what the managing director of the shipping line has commanded them to do. But below the water line are many hidden costs that are not generally measured by companies.

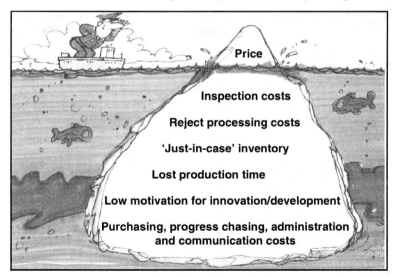

Figure 33

Besides the cost of internal inspection, discussed earlier, there are many other costs that should be identified: reject-processing costs, just-in-case inventories (because you are never sure if your supplier is going to supply a quality product on time), associated lost production time, purchasing costs, progress costs, accounts administration costs, and so on, including the very high cost of remedial action when things have gone wrong.

Unfortunately, I have seen too many purchasing departments in British industry where the people appear to have an inadequate training in such basic requirements as cost accountancy. They are often unfamiliar with statistical process control and with many other tools of total quality management. They certainly tend to have little understanding of the cost of quality.

The good news is that things are changing. Much more effort is being made by the professional bodies to raise quality standards within the field of purchasing, which has now finally been allowed to emerge from the back room and been acknowledged as one of the most vital areas within any organisation.

Finding and Keeping Top-Class Suppliers

So, how do we go about finding all these wonderful new suppliers that are out there? First we conduct some trial business with suppliers using ISO 9000 or similar vendorrating assessment techniques. If the trial is successful, we then assemble a multi-functional team to assess the new supplier. The team reviews all aspects of the company's performance: Is the paperwork neat and tidily presented? Does it arrive on time? Is it understandable? Is it accurate? What is the supplier like on the telephone? How well do they respond to problems?

The team members also review the technical aspects of the supplier's products and the supplier's attitude to the team itself – how cooperative and proactive they are. We have a weighted factor of 30 per cent of the results of the assessment associated with the culture of the company. We want suppliers who are like Dutton Engineering. It is no good working with suppliers whose culture is out of line with our own.

Quality and on-time delivery are rated at 25 per cent each. Price is rated at only 20 per cent. This often amazes other business people, but our experience has shown that if any of the other three elements are not in line, the apparent price benefits are illusory, because working with such companies always costs us more anyway.

Figure 34 contrasts traditional practice (where lowest price is dominant) with partnership sourcing in Figure 35. If you go down the former route you have to have inspection in place to check on product quality. With the traditional route, if suppliers perform badly, you just change them and continue to change them. Often, however, the new ones prove to be even worse than the previous ones. In addition, you must ensure that you renegotiate at regular intervals with a view to seeing if you can screw the supplier down even more or kick up a fuss about his quality and delivery performance.

Other key aspects of such a relationship are that you keep the supplier at arm's length telling them very little and holding all your cards to your chest. Confidentiality is the watchword. Such relationships are win/lose – either you win and they lose, or vice versa.

Partnership sourcing marks a totally different way of doing things. Here, the dominant criterion is total cost. Our

PARTNERSHIP SOURCING
TRADITIONAL PRACTICE vs PARTNERSHIP SOURCING
OLD

- Price is dominant
- Check product quality
- Poor performance, change supplier
- Renegotiate at regular intervals
- Win/Lose relationship

Figure 34

PARTNERSHIP SOURCING
TRADITIONAL PRACTICE vs PARTNERSHIP SOURCING
NEW

- Total cost is dominant
- Assured quality
- Offer preventative help, pool resources
- Build firm relationship
- Teamwork to improve competitiveness
- Win/Win relationship
- Mutual profitability

Figure 35

measurements have proved indisputably that it makes financial sense. Now, even our accountants are convinced! Quality becomes assured. Preventive help becomes part of the norm and resources are pooled. Firm and lasting relationships are created, and the developing team work will act to improve both companies' competitiveness. Such a relationship is win/win, with both companies benefiting both financially and socially (Figure 36).

Figure 36

All these changes of attitude towards trading with your suppliers can only be based on trust, and developing this can sometimes take a long time for both parties. Once the process is under way, however, and the relationship starts to develop, the benefits to both companies soon start to flow. Confidence grows and bolder and bolder steps are taken. The competitive force thus unleashed is very powerful indeed. It will engender an atmosphere in which both supplier and customer will be able to eliminate the massive amounts of wasted time and resources bound up in traditional processes – processes once considered absolutely fundamental for running any business.

An important improvement will be your just-in-case stock pile (Figure 37), which is in truth just a comfort factor that you will no longer require. On my journeys around British industry, I am truly staggered at the amount of stores and stock items that are still retained – often only because they make the balance sheet look healthy. Goods are only of value if you can sell them. If you cannot sell them, they are a liability. They take up very valuable space and, moreover, when you want that left-hand widget you bought two years ago, you generally cannot even find it amongst all the stock. You waste lots of time looking and eventually still end up having to go out and buy another one.

Figure 37

Much of this stock has probably come from that 'wonderful' minimum order charge, which obliges you to buy 20 times more than you really need. In my company, I adopt the principle that, if we cannot sell it within four weeks, we ought to throw it away. This I often do, to the dismay of some of my 'magpie' colleagues.

As I mentioned earlier, paying your suppliers on time is fundamental to partnership sourcing. If you do not pay on time, you will never develop the right kind of relationship with your suppliers (Figure 38). We always agree on terms with our suppliers from the outset. Then we adhere religiously to those terms of trading. It is particularly important for larger companies to ensure that they pay their smaller suppliers on time, since a two- to three-month wait for payment can often plunge small companies into a very difficult financial position.

Figure 38

Traditional methods of purchasing and supply often create that terrifying character, the paper monster (Figure 39). Our experience at Dutton is that paper is simply a comfort factor that adds nothing of any value to the business. Most of it comes from outdated systems that should have been changed years ago.

Figure 39

Partnership sourcing will eliminate a large number of these wasteful paper documents. We, for example, have managed to reduce the number of purchase invoices processed by our company each month from nearly 200 to 60 (Figure 40). The beauty of our situation is that even if we double or treble the amount of business with these suppliers, we still will not have more than approximately 60 invoices a month. This means that we will not need to employ additional staff to shuffle the additional paper around.

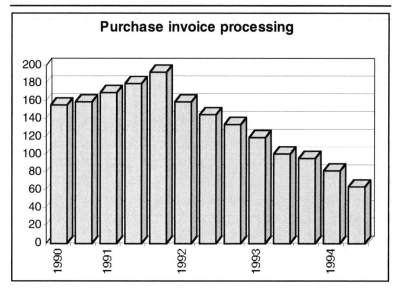

Figure 40

Our single-sourcing policy has streamlined our activities very considerably (Figure 41). In 1991, we saw a substantial

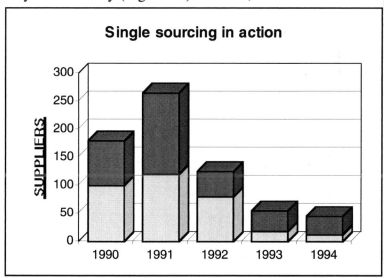

Figure 41

growth in the company and had more than 250 suppliers. In 1992, we thought we had reduced our supply chain to the optimum level when we hit the 100 mark. However, we reduced the number still further by looking at our best suppliers.

For example, our nut and bolt supplier was so good that we asked him if he could supply our polishing consumables. This represented a whole new business area for him to set up; but he did it, and he has now expanded the range he can offer to the rest of his customer base. It helped him, and it helped us to condense our range of suppliers still further.

We have now just under 50 suppliers, with a core of 10. I doubt if we shall be able to reduce it much more: it is, after all, highly unlikely that our stationery supplier will be able to supply us with our steel.

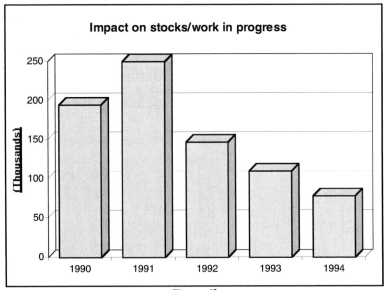

Figure 42

Partnership sourcing and *Kanbans* had a dramatic effect on our stock and work in progress (Figure 42). This declined from the 1991 level of over £250,000 to the 1992 level of £150,000. In 1993, we reduced it to just over £100,000 by the introduction of lean manufacture, whereby we make one when we have sold one. Annual hours (see below) brought us a great surprise when the figure fell one month to £89,000. And all this despite the fact that, over those four years, our sales had increased by 50 per cent. The secret was that we pulled material only in when we needed it.

We are still continuing to develop and improve our supply chain. At present we are working with our suppliers to introduce computers and information technology with a view to becoming a paperless business within three years. What is clear is that we need our suppliers on board with us, thinking the same way we do. At Dutton, if our suppliers continue to demonstrate the same commitment to our company as they do at present, they will be on board for life.

Partnership sourcing can and should have an enormous impact on your company; but it needs some brave decisions to be taken, as well as absolute support from top management to see the whole project through.

6

The Way Forward
2 – Team Working

In the Western world, and certainly in the UK, we are not very good at team working. Our entire society is built around the achievement of the individual. Our education system, from primary school through to university, focuses on personal achievement. Out in the commercial world, rates of pay, promotions and privileges are all geared to individual performance. Small wonder then that few of us are natural team players.

Many companies are guilty of the pigeon-hole syndrome – creating a working framework that tends to leave people with very little understanding of what happens outside their own departments. Fortunately, this is finally beginning to change. It is now becoming increasingly understood and accepted that *personal* excellence alone is not enough, and that to achieve *business* excellence within an organisation there has to be a real team effort.

This focus on team performance is an inherent part of some cultures. Japan, for example, is of a nation of team players and we in the West are now looking at ways of bringing team work into our organisations. The question is: 'Where do we start?'.

Here again, my view is that we should return to the basic proposition that everyone in our organisation is full of talent and has a vital part to play in the day-to-day efficient and effective running of our companies. By itself, individual excellence will not necessarily ensure quality products nor on-time deliveries. On the contrary, when we become too focused on our individual contribution, we tend to lose sight of the requirements of our internal customers – our colleagues who depend on us to be able to fulfil their own roles properly.

To change this approach within a company, organisation or country represents major cultural change, and depends on good leadership. Even at Dutton, in a company employing less than 30 people, we had somehow managed to become 'departmentalised'. This had never been a conscious decision; it had evolved over time and was in danger of becoming entrenched. On the manufacturing side, in particular, we had developed skill centres – a welding shop, a fabricating shop, and a polishing shop, each of which had its own supervisor, typically the most highly-skilled person.

Within these departments, our people had carefully focused job descriptions and they were often permanently restricted to one machine or to one particular area of activity (Figure 43). This gave rise to a situation in which everyone ran around independently doing what they thought was a wonderful job (Figure 44).

Figure 43   *Figure 44*

We decided that this situation should be radically restructured to bring the skills and efforts more into line (Figure 45). Thus, at the outset of our total quality journey we resolved to develop a team of much more flexible and multi-skilled employees (Figure 46).

Figure 45   *Figure 46*

Since training had always been one of Dutton's strengths (we had always given everyone the opportunity to learn new skills), we carried out an audit and identified a dozen core skills. A few people were skilled in more than one area and we adopted a target for every person to have at least three core skills, and preferably many more. We devised a simple, visual, skills matrix, which was placed on the factory wall, and allocated employees cards whenever they achieved a particular skill. A certain useful personal rivalry then crept in, and many employees developed themselves into whole new skill areas.

This evolution towards multi-skilling went a long way towards eliminating the previous problems of skill shortages and bottlenecks that always seemed to crop up during employee holidays or sick leave.

Although within the company as a whole a sense of genuine team spirit was beginning to evolve, we nevertheless needed to raise our sights much higher. On the factory floor, our products still used to go through everyone's hands, and there was therefore very little personal ownership of quality. Thus, we identified two vital issues – customer partnership and product quality – that we had to focus upon. This was to combat the attitude that when the product was out of any one individual's hands, it was no longer his job. We had to get our people closer to our external customers and also to develop a better understanding in-house of what everyone's internal customers needed. We took the view that teamwork would come to give us the ability to improve, and so we completely reorganised the production system, creating two multi-functional teams.

Each team encompassed the whole gamut of skills: punching, welding, fabrication, polishing, etc. The post of supervisor disappeared to be replaced by that of team leader, of which we had two. The team leaders were to act as guides and coaches to their teams, while encouraging as much devolution of responsibility as possible. We went for the change in January of 1993, finishing at Christmas shutdown as departments and resuming in the New Year as teams. If only it could have been that simple!

Teams in Place

Having set up our teams, we looked at the pattern of work going through the factory at the time. We saw that about 80 per cent of our sales was through partnership relations with our largest customers. The rest was 'jobbing' work. We therefore shared out the 80 per cent of expected work between the teams, dividing it according to product line or customer, so that one team would focus on one or other product. This meant that products would no longer need to pass through the whole factory.

It was here that we met the initial resistance. The first few weeks brought with them a lot of dissatisfaction and protests that many members of staff would rather return to the old ways of doing things. Since people often feel uncomfortable with change, and can indeed often feel quite threatened by it, this came as no great surprise to us. But training was once again the key, together with proper communication, so that everyone came to understand and firmly support the reasons behind the change and the goals.

Team building

At Dutton we used a number of techniques to try to build our teams, some of which proved more successful than others. We started by having each team attend a half-hour sit-down meeting every Monday morning. We asked each team to identify things that were going well in the company and things that were not going so well. One issue of dissatisfaction that emerged early on was the disparity that existed in rates of pay (this was a factor which was taken into consideration later when we moved to annual hours). These meetings proved to be a salutary lesson: you cannot simply take a group of eight people, put them in a room, and tell them they are a team. They won't be.

It took us some time and considerable training to discover that besides a balance of technical skills, every team also needs a balance of personalities. Team leaders, for example, needed training in complex interpersonal skills, something that was new territory for them.

Initially, we got the two new team leaders to undertake a variety of leadership and team-building courses to help them understand their new role. We also indulged in a few interesting self-analysis exercises to find out who among us were 'visionaries', 'creatives', 'cynics', 'doers', etc. The team leaders experimented on the management team first, and we were pleased to see that at the time we had one person in each of the four categories. They then tried the same thing on their team colleagues, and it was at that point that we started to recognise the strengths and weaknesses of the two teams.

Soon the weekly half-hour team meetings were abandoned at the suggestion of the employees themselves. They saw the time spent as 'unproductive' and therefore wasted. We later adopted the stance that the daily meetings should be 'ten minutes on your feet, not half an hour on your seat'. This was remarkably successful in terms of keeping the focus on the main points rather than on the usual cup of coffee, on the previous night's TV programmes, and so forth.

The teams slowly began to establish themselves, selecting an area of the factory for their large wipe-board to record day-to-day information on new orders and work in hand. Team leaders and team members went out to visit the customers whose orders they were manufacturing, often spending time working on the customers' assembly lines side by side with their customers' own staff. They began to feel much closer to our customers, and over a period of months the teams developed a real feeling of ownership of the products that they were making. They were also now working with team members with quite different skills from their own and started to have a better understanding of the whole job process. This certainly proved the old adage that the more pieces of the jigsaw one can see, the better job one makes of completing the picture.

We found that people were enjoying the opportunity both to learn and to pass on new skills. Multi-skilling became a way of life. This benefited both the company and the individuals, who now could look forward to far less monotony in their day-to-day work.

Next, we wondered about how to identify the teams, and we left this question up to the teams themselves. Novelties like the 'speedy' team and the 'champion' team were bandied about for a while and rejected. They finally opted for simple colours: the Red team and the Green team. Naturally, it was only a matter of weeks before the teams enquired whether Dutton would buy them coloured polo shirts in team colours. I still think this had something to do with the fact that the management team had difficulty in remembering who was in which team. Now the team members all wear their coloured shirts with pride, and if on the odd day a team member forgets to put on his shirt, he can expect some serious leg-pulling from his colleagues.

By early 1995, we had added a Blue team, and with expansion in the air more teams look likely to follow. Teams seem to work well if kept to around eight members, and so, as the company grows, we would prefer to create new teams rather than increase the size of existing ones.

I should also add that as much responsibility as possible is kept in the hands of the team. Management simply provides the resources and support for day-to-day functional needs. Decisions on manufacturing techniques, job allocation, choice of consumables and work scheduling are left entirely to team leaders. This means that their job is far more comprehensive than that ever dealt with by a supervisor.

They are highly involved with the purchase of materials and consumables, with customers and suppliers, and they provide a vital support for the management team strategy.

Each team in turn is encouraged not to look upwards to the team leader for instructions, but to have the confidence to take decisions for themselves (Figure 47). Naturally, all this was very new at first, and some of our less-confident employees needed moral and practical support during this learning period to give them the courage to tackle the increased level of personal responsibility.

Figure 47

In moving to team working, we achieved the following bene-fits and advantages:

- Knowledge of all areas within one team
- Specialised focus on one product
- Team ownership of the product

- One-to-one customer liaison
- Increased training potential.

Over the years, we have learnt that successful teamworking requires the following:

- The right atmosphere within the company
- The right kind of leadership offering direction and control
- Technical knowledge and developed interpersonal skills
- Established work methods and routines.

Several months into team working we had the confidence to look again at our working methods and practices with a view to improving our flexibility still further. Our goal was not simply to manufacture 'just in time', but to move onwards to true lean manufacturing.

This was a huge step change from the old philosophy of nice big production batches for maximum machine efficiency. For us, lean manufacturing meant that we should aim for 'sell one, make one'. The resulting smaller and smaller batches meant that we would require different ways of operating in the factory, and we thought we might have come across an exciting new strategy when we first heard about the system of annual hours.

Annual Hours

Annual hours is a fairly new concept in Britain, being currently practised by only 14 per cent or so of UK companies, mostly those involved with seasonal products or services. The first insight we had was through a magazine article published about the remarkable changes taking place in a company called Bomford Turner, based in the South of England. They make equipment for contract and roadside grass cutting and hedge trimming and, as might be expected, they saw large seasonal fluctuations in their work load. They always worked very long hours in the summer and had little to occupy their highly skilled workforce during the winter months.

To adjust to this work pattern, Bomford Turner adopted a system of annual hours. Under this scheme, the paid weekly contract for a fixed number of hours was replaced by a paid annual contract for a fixed number of hours. Hours were then rostered so that employees would work long weeks in the busy summer months and short weeks during the quiet winter period.

At Dutton, however, our order book is not seasonably predictable, something that I suspect is a great problem for most other businesses. We never actually know what our customers are going to want or when they are going to want it. The only certainty that exists is that, once the customers place the order, they want a speedy response.

Before annual hours, Dutton operated a 39-hour week for its production operatives, who were all hourly paid. We worked this over a four-day week – Monday to Thursday. This left Friday and Saturday for overtime, if work dictated. Typically, we would have periods of low orders, and in the old days we would simply pull some material in and start a batch of goods for one or other of our partnership customers, with the expectation that they would soon be needing them anyway. Or we painted the floor, or did some maintenance, or whatever. Sometimes, people would simply stretch the work out to fill the day, knowing that this was the only work on hand. Naturally, this had the effect of throwing out any 'time on job' calculations – something we are very hot on at Dutton. Then we would find ourselves in the midst of a very busy period – and of course the customer invariably did not want the items that we had just built a large batch of. He wanted something else. And he wanted it yesterday! This would inevitably lead to people running around like lunatics and laying on lots of overtime.

This was not lean manufacturing, just-in-time, or anything like it. So we took a long hard look at our organisation and discovered the universal truth about virtually all businesses: they are like a juggling act. To be able to do your job, you need five things to be in place (Figure 48). These are:

- A purchase order, or work instructions
- Detailed information or a drawing showing exactly what is required
- A piece of plant, equipment or computer on which to perform the task
- Raw materials (steel, plastics, cloth, data, etc.)
- A person skilled in the task.

Figure 48

If any of these five essential components are not in place, then someone, somewhere in your organisation, is left twiddling their thumbs. The thing is that they usually twiddle away invisibly. People do not dare let their colleagues know that they have nothing to do. People shuffle paper, stroll around, look busy, or even go walkabout. If there is one missing piece in the jigsaw, then people are unable to spend their time productively.

We wanted to find ways of eliminating these areas of wasted time, which were not only a cost to the company, but often represented a source of great frustration for the employees themselves.

Annual hours seemed to be the solution, and we therefore spent a year looking at it in action in various companies, examining how they had implemented it and what might be the possible benefits and pitfalls. We had come to dislike barriers and restrictions, and we therefore looked at adopting annual hours in its simplest form. The basic requirement would be to work 1770 hours per year, calculated from 52 weeks at 39 hours minus 195 hours' holidays and 64 hours' Bank Holidays. There would also be a possible reserve of a further 160 hours that could be called upon – a figure calculated on the basis of the average of overtime worked during the preceding three years.

The basic outline was therefore:

Annual basic requirement: 1770 hours
Reserve: 160 hours.

The reserves were intended to be used for sickness, medical or dental appointments, rework, and peak production.

We made it plain that no one would be working more than 1770 hours plus the 160. We also promoted the idea that, by working smart, staff could expect to work fewer hours. In return for this annual contract everyone would go onto monthly salary.

Working hours were to be according to customer demand, and during slack periods a short week would therefore be worked; and during busy periods a long week (Figure 49). No fixed rules were laid down, but we did have a few guidelines for ourselves and our employees. The details of the proposal appear in Appendix 1.

Figure 49

Having spent quite some time looking at the options, we arranged for our lawyers to draw up a new contract of employment. This was a wonderful opportunity for us to achieve something which I aspired to for a long time: *a single-status company.*

The new contract abolished the differences between people who had traditionally been hourly paid and those who had been paid monthly. Everyone was now to have exactly the same terms and conditions of employment, sickness benefits, pension rights, etc. We also tore up the old job descriptions, believing them to be far too restrictive. We now only have two job descriptions at Dutton: Production Operative and Administration Operative.

There was token resistance from one or two people whose previous contracts were 'Skilled ... Operator', but this resistance quickly evaporated when the entire management team made it clear that they too had abandoned the restrictive practices of the past.

Such a step change can only be implemented successfully with full support, and so we spent much time in preparation before putting the issue of adopting annual hours to the vote by all members of staff. Naturally, it has to be admitted that there were winners and losers. The salary we set was equal for all production operatives, which lifted some employees way above their previous income levels. No one lost out on their basic pay, but as in any environment where overtime exists there were a privileged few who had always enjoyed high levels of overtime. This overtime was effectively being abolished, and this meant that some people would potentially receive less money than they were used to earning at the year end.

When the vote was taken, only two employees voted against (Figure 50). The majority won out and elected to start the new system on 1 April 1994, to tie in with the start of the new tax year.

When it came to signing the new contracts, we made sure that every employee received individual counselling and understood the full implications of the new regime. To our surprise, even the two employees who had voted against annual hours opted to sign the new contracts and they stayed with us for a period of several months of annual hours before deciding that the new Dutton was not for them and leaving for pastures new.

Figure 50

But why were so many of the others so keen to buy into the new system? One of the reasons was the new pay structure. We had previously managed to get ourselves into a situation where we were paying 13 different rates of pay across 22 employees, and, as you might imagine, this did not sit well with multi-skilling, team working and equal sharing of responsibility (Figure 51).

Figure 51

119

At the time we were pretty certain that team working would take some time to bed down, so we thought that eradicating pay differentials would help overcome the problems. Thus, for the first year we put everyone onto one equal rate of pay. Over the next year, however, we discovered that it is very important to recognise the achievement of the individual, and, in 1995, we implemented a formal appraisal system, with three grades of pay.

Our approach was to create an assessment 'scorecard' addressing many of the motivational and team qualities of the employee rather than just focusing on technical ability. Consideration was given to willingness to learn new skills, and to cooperate to with other team members. We also used the appraisal process to set each person individual targets and areas for improvement, with the knowledge that on the next quarterly appraisal they might be able achieve a higher grade.

Managing Annual Hours

So, how did we set about managing annual hours? The crucial element was that management tried to be involved as little as possible. The only requirement was that the teams deliver their products to the customer on time, with the right quality. Once they had completed their tasks they were free to go home. This would mean that, if they worked smart, they would be able to enjoy more leisure time, something that acted as a real spur.

We kept the same core hours as previously worked, but the teams had the freedom to choose their own working patterns, coming in early or working late according to customer requirements. In fact, people tend to be creatures of habit, and most people still stick to the same 7.30 to 5.45 timetable that they have always done.

However, it is the teams that manage their own work flow as a group. Typically, on a Monday morning they will have a team meeting, with all the team members standing at the wipe-board showing the details of orders and delivery requirements (Figure 52). The team members know what is needed to fulfil these requirements. Some of our products will need to go through a single work centre; some might go through half a dozen work centres and out to subcontractors. It is the team members who liaise with the customers and suppliers to ensure that the work runs smoothly.

Figure 52

During the initial few weeks of annual hours the teams took some interesting decisions. One Monday morning, the steel stockholder's transport broke down and the material failed to arrive as expected. Under the old regime, everyone would have tidied up, swept the floor, and generally made themselves look busy until going home time. Instead, the team took the decision to go home for the day and to ensure that the work was done by coming in early on a couple of mornings and working late on other days during the week.

Figure 53

Annual hours has meant that the time spent at work has come to be used much more effectively. There is no longer an incentive to stretch work to fit the day. The new incentive is to finish the work and go home (Figure 53). (The downside, of course, is that at times the team members will have to work into the night, but this is a trade-off and is understood by all and accepted – Figure 54.)

Figure 54

The difference in performance has been incredible to behold. It is as if a whole bunch of magic wands has been found. Efficiency leapt up beyond all our expectations.

At Dutton, we have found that annual hours has put the last piece of the jigsaw in place. Our teams are now not only facing in the same direction; they are now focused correctly and all pulling together (Figure 55).

Many visitors to our company have asked with concern about how we deal with urgent orders that arrive after the teams have gone home early. How, they want to know, do we maintain the strong customer focus? Since we began annual hours, firefighting is mostly a thing of the past within Dutton and there have only been a few occasions when undue actions have been called for. However, there must always be a solution for every eventuality and ours came about after one visitor to the company felt so enthusiastic about the level of teamwork at Dutton that he wanted to 'treat' the work-force. The team concerned opted to use the gift to buy a bleeper, and this proved so popular an idea that we bought one for each team. Team members now take turns to take the bleeper home.

The value of the solution proved itself conclusively shortly afterwards. One week, having satisfied all their customers' needs by the Wednesday lunchtime, the Blue

Team went home. On the Friday morning, however, one of their customers rang in to say that they had forgotten to order some brackets for machines that were due for despatch that weekend. We phoned in to the Blue Team's bleeper, only to find the bleeper holder in London ensconced at McDonald's in Oxford Street. The team member immediately found a phone and rang into the office. Grasping the situation immediately, the bleeper holder referred to the list of the team's phone numbers, which is also kept with the bleeper, and began to ring around to draw together a team with the skills to manufacture the component. The first call revealed that the team member sought was playing golf and could not be contacted. The second call, however, reached a sheet-metal-worker, who undertook to track down a specialist welder from his own team. Within 20 minutes, both members of the team were at the factory ready to manufacture the components. One and a half hours later, the team members had made and carefully wrapped the components; had produced the delivery paperwork; and had delivered the items to their customer on their way home. Such is the level of customer service that our teams now offer!

Cell Manufacture

In Japan, I was most impressed by just how well the Japanese laid out their factories, and, as time went by, and with it our continual quest to improve, we decided to look more closely at cell manufacturing. As always with new projects we set out to research the state of play within the UK by visiting other companies, both big and small, to learn the pluses and minuses of this approach to manufacturing.

We also looked at a variety of training courses - one

lasting four days, the other two - and selected particular members of the teams to go on them. Ron Larter, the Red Team leader, was selected for the four-day course organised by the Kaizen Institute at Premier Exhausts in Coventry, and I take great delight in periodically playfully reminding him that this training cost the company £2,000. The trainees were from both the UK and America, and the programme was led by some Japanese instructors.

The first two days were spent on the philosophy of cell manufacturing. The rest of the time was spent on the shop floor, which was operating at full tilt, putting the theory into practice. Thus, besides having to cope with the problem of creating the best plant layout to achieve their goals, the trainees also had to win over the Premier Exhausts employees to accept the changes they were proposing. After identifying the optimum layouts, the teams spent the day discussing the issues and reaching generalised agreement. Then, overnight, the equipment was moved around by contractors, so that the next day could actually be spent by the trainees testing out their proposals in practice. The first 24 hours gave rise to significant improvements, but, after the rearrangement, the work force remained somewhat unconvinced.

At the end of the course, however, the trainees managed to achieve most of their objectives. The most staggering result was that lead time per part fell from 180 minutes to a mere three! Introduction of a *Kanban* system brought stock levels down, and the engineer's ultimate goal of one-piece flow was also achieved.

There were congratulations all round before everyone began to leave for their respective companies. Then, up popped a vital question from one of the operatives who had to work within the new layout and system. Where, he asked with a smile, could he put his cup of coffee? It just goes to emphasise that, in such reorganisations, every aspect must be reviewed and everyone consulted - a vital issue that the trainees had omitted to consider!

Jack Gray from our Green Team went off for a two-day, classroom-based course. Upon his return, Jack decided to calculate how far our teams would have to carry our components per year with the existing layout. The result? Some 800 miles! So, our external training complete, we arranged for the whole company to spend a day building model Lego cars under the guidance of a good friend of ours, George Harlock of Triangle Implementations. The aim of the activity was to achieve an agreed price and an agreed production rate. By the end of the day, having laid out their cells on a flip chart for the first time, the team had learnt a good many lessons and were able to put the ideas straight into practice. Many more hours were then spent until the teams were completely satisfied with their initial layouts. The plant and equipment were moved around over the Christmas period and, at the same time, over 300 further Kaizen improvements were carried out.

A mere two weeks later, the Green Team was actually operating with one-piece flow, reducing the distance that the components would have to travel by almost 300%! The 600 or so miles walking that this new layout saved could thus be used by the team members on the golf course or strolling along the river.

But the teams have not stopped there. They continue to work on their layouts, tweaking this or that as the products continue to mature.

Our visitors often ask us how we maintain discipline at Dutton. My view is that discipline is maintained indirectly by our customers, those whom we are trying to satisfy and delight. However, on a day-to-day level, we have found that peer pressure is the most effective disciplining force. It is certainly far more effective than management pressure in terms of ensuring that all team members are performing to the best of their abilities.

Only on one occasion, in the very earliest days of team working at Dutton, have I ever been asked by one of the teams to speak to a member who, in their opinion, was underperforming and unprepared to go the extra mile for his team. I called him into my office, told him of the team's concerns regarding his performance, and asked him to talk through any problems he might have. Unsatisfied by his response and rather taken aback that such an attitude should persist at Dutton, I decided to suspend him on full pay for three days to give him the chance to reflect on his relationship with his colleagues and with the company.

Three days later, back he came into my office. What, I demanded to know, had he to say for himself? Firstly, he said, those three days had been the worst three days of his life. Not only had he not been sure that he had a job to return to; but the main thing - something that almost bowled me over - was that he had missed his team mates and had realised that he had let them down. Off he went to apologise.

That was the first and only time in my career that I have ever actually seen anyone change in three days. And the upshot? This young man has gone onto perform superbly within the company, and he is now a very valuable member of Dutton. In fact, on a recent visit to one of his customers, he picked up an enquiry for £300,000 worth of work, which was converted into a firm order.

So, now we see round us colleagues who are enjoying a significant improvement in the quality of their lives, both at home and at work. Dutton has been transformed into a stimulating and challenging environment. We have become a learning organisation in which our people are encouraged to search for knowledge, both inside and outside the company. For instance, you can do any course that interests you and the company will pay for it. Nobody has taken up Needlepoint; most of the areas they are following up at evening classes are linked to increasing their computer skills or to language learning, both of which, of course, benefit the company. But the choice is theirs. More importantly, as individuals, our team members are all starting to learn again. In my view, this is one of the great problems facing British industry. All too many managers - especially owner-managers of smaller companies - have stopped learning. Perhaps they don't feel they can spare the time to go out and see the great changes that are taking place around them. My view, however, is that, unless managers cast aside all outmoded mental patterns, they will continue to spend their working lives firefighting and groping in the dark for solutions.

It is a truism that knowledge is power and we are often asked why we at Dutton are prepared to share both our experience and the lessons we have learned over the last few years. Our view is that knowledge is only valuable when shared.

So, I would say to my colleagues in the UK's small to medium sized enterprises: Take up the challenge of change; don't leave it till next week before you start. Do it now! That first small step is the most important. And, is it worth doing? Well, it is up to you to judge.

7

Results

As mentioned earlier, at Dutton we now have multi-functional teams able to manufacture a product from start to finish, and team members who have been trained in cost accountancy, who deal direct with their customers and look after their needs. (At this point, I feel I must mention that it takes over five years to train fabricator/welders to do their jobs, while it only takes 2½ hours to teach them cost accountancy!) The result is that we have moved a long way towards team budget setting. We are now using activity-based costing throughout the company. This has itself acted as a very powerful tool for continuous improvement. For example, since each team produces delivery notes and invoices for finished goods, the costs of producing delivery notes and invoices are now apportioned accordingly. Thus, teams that produce a lot of delivery notes and invoices need to budget more than teams that produce only a few. One of our teams, for example, has a customer who requires only one invoice a month; so the team's share of these administration costs is relatively small. This has encouraged the other teams to look at cost reduction in this area.

The teams also pay a proportion of the cost of the floor space, including storage, that they need to operate in. One team has therefore been prompted to build upwards to help reduce the costs incurred in running their operations. Clearly this is an area of diminishing returns, but it certainly helps team members focus on the continual cost (and hence price) reductions that global competition is forcing upon us. They are being actively drawn into the process of improving their efficiency and effectiveness.

As part of their budgeting, each of our teams produces a six-month rolling forecast.

As managing director, I need the following information:

- *What the teams estimate their sales will be for that period*
- *What the estimated return will be.*

It is then up to the teams to go out and find out from their customers what they intend to spend over that six-month period. Knowing what the sales budget is likely to be, as well as their share of the fixed costs, the teams are well on their way to setting their own salaries.

Over the past few years, we have moved from everybody in the teams being on the same salary to having three grades; but we have now concluded that the way forward is self-set salaries. There are a number of reasons for this, but primarily it is because pay has always been an area of immense emotion and divisiveness. Dissatisfaction in this field can poison any atmosphere, destroy job satisfaction, cloud judgement, and definitely damage the chances for the future success of any company.

So, how will we go about instigating self-set salaries?

Well, we will start by looking at what the market can stand. This will be derived from what our sales are likely to be and what our costs are. The remainder will be divided up into salaries.

In general, from a management view, there are some things that I know, such as: what salaries are being paid to everybody in the company, and what salaries are being paid outside in the market place for similar jobs. What I don't know are things about the individual employees' requirements, such as: how much money they need to pay their bills, and how much is being earned by the people that they went to school with or that they meet socially. Furthermore, I also do not know what aspirations they have: do they want a new house, a foreign holiday, a new car, etc.? In our society, egos are very much bound up with salaries and your earnings tend very much to reflect, (both to yourself and to others) whether you are getting on or not in your career.

Since I know what I know, but not those things that are important to our team members, all I need to do is to give them the two things I know for them to be able to make an informed decision regarding their salaries. The figure they derive will then prove to be realistic or otherwise.

In my discussions with others outside Dutton, some have suggested that employees will tend just to rush off and double or treble their salaries. In our pilot experiment I have found this not to be the case. If you have been a reasonable employer, your staff will already be getting salaries that reflect the market place for their particular job. And the advantages to all will be considerable: firstly, each team member then will have a vested interest in reducing waste within their operations, and hence within the company in general. This will reinforce the focus on the teams' ability to satisfy or, better still, delight the customer. In any event, tying improved incomes to performance will certainly help concentrate the teams' minds on how to improve and to reduce costs. We shall see how this develops.

The Recession Hits

Clearly, however, at Dutton we are not immune to the fate of the wider economy; in 1996, after a year in which our sales grew by 48 per cent, we experienced a three-month period of dramatically falling sales in our business with one of our main customers. We started to incur losses month by month. So, as per usual, I called everyone together and asked their views on what we ought to do about the situation. After a general discussion, the teams went off to come up with some solutions. Imagine my surprise when they returned and offered to take a pay cut, so as to stop the haemorrhage of money out of the business, until we could come up with a more permanent solution. In I plunged with a lead. "Well," I said, "if you agree to a pay cut, I will double it in terms of my own income." Off they went to discuss the matter, returning shortly afterwards to recommend a 10% cut. Thank goodness they didn't opt for 50%!

I then asked the teams to go away and reset their budgets for the next six months, since, given the scale of decline in the business, the pay cut would not really tackle the situation in full. After two days, back they came to announce that they were unable to get their figures to stack up in any way so as to show any reasonable return. The real problem, they said, lay in that they had too many people in their teams. (This must be seen in the context that, over the past few years, we had moved from having 40 people producing £1 million to 26 people producing £2 million of sales; and yet here they were saying we still had three or four people too many!) So, I asked them to propose a solution. Once again, they came up with a solution: to go away and see if anyone wanted to leave.

The upshot was that three people were prepared to take voluntary redundancy. As it turned out, one team member had always wanted to be a civil servant; another never really seemed to be at home with this way of running an organisation and took the opportunity to leave; and the third person had problems with travel arrangements and this also appeared to be a solution for him. We also decided to send one of our younger people off for on 12-month course at an engineering training centre.

Having come up with a solution, the teams immediately reset their salaries to their original levels.

Naturally, this approach has resulted in the teams coming up with ways of containing expenses that I could never have applied myself. I saw this in action some months later. Entering the factory one morning, I saw a young man I did not recognise standing there. In response to my request, back came the answer from the team: "Oh, he's part of our cost-cutting programme! We've got him working for us for £3.00 per hour". I was horrified, commenting that it was outright exploitation. Back came the response that he was the son of one of the team members, a student on holiday, who was delighted to have the chance to earn a bit of money. What could I do but shake my head? Looking back later, I remembered having suggested several times bringing in temporary labour to help us through our peak working periods. And the response then? "By the time we've trained them, it will be time for them to leave." Somehow, if the solutions are mine, they are considered unworkable. If they come from the team, they usually seem to work. Funny how the 'not invented here' syndrome gets everywhere!

What is more, now the teams actively seek additional work from their existing customer base. As already mentioned, they have brought back orders worth well over £300,000. This has confirmed to team members that opportunities exist with the customer base for each of them to take. Long gone are those days when they thought that their customers would only want to deal with a manager. Now each team is in a position to offer their customers what they want.

When I was attempting to get the teams to appreciate that I wanted them to be able to take increasing responsibility for their customers' satisfaction, I told them what had happened to me shortly beforehand at my local branch of Marks & Spencer, where I had gone to change a shirt. Inside the store, I found a member of staff who, without needing to call a manager, took control and immediately remedied the problem to my great satisfaction. If, I told the teams, staff at Marks & Spencer can offer such excellent service without reference to a manager, then why shouldn't we? The lesson has been well learnt in Dutton and the result has brought our company tremendous competitive advantage.

So, now I truly believe that Dutton is getting into shape for the 21st century. This is absolutely necessary, it is becoming clearer by the day. And yet, wearing the hat of Chairman of the Bedfordshire TEC, I often find myself asking why so many people and so many companies are resisting change. The answer, I suggest, is very much linked to fear, jealousy, greed and envy, and to holding on to personal status and control – all the things that customers are no longer prepared to pay for and that make our lives so much more complex and difficult. The question remains: how long can our companies survive without fundamental change?

Perhaps the way forward is to communicate to more and more companies and organisations some of the benefits of change. Below are some of the business results these changes have had on Dutton's performance in 1995/96:

- Sales increased by 48% within 12 months
- Lead times (on any of our five models of ink-jet printer housings) fell from 6 weeks to 8 hours
- Kaizen (small improvements by everyone involved) has reduced our machine set-up times from 90 minutes to 8 minutes
- Rejects have fallen from 10% to 0.7% (mainly surface scratches caused in transit)
- On-time deliveries have risen from 60% to 99.4%
- Stock turns in some cells have risen from 4 to 125
- Sales per employee are twice the average for our industry.

Furthermore, prior to 1995, our company was in the red, with an overdraft of £¼ million. The Dutton of today is now solidly in the black. For us it has all been worthwhile and I am convinced that this approach has something to offer other companies.

Without a doubt, the future will hold many more challenges for Dutton. There remains a long way to go. However, with everyone in the company being clearly focused and moving together in the right direction, I am confident that Dutton will remain a healthy and vibrant firm, a good place to work, where individual abilities and interests can be developed to the full and, in terms of performance, a formidable force to be reckoned with.

8

The Future

The one certain thing about the future is that it will not be the same as today. Having embarked on our total quality journey, we have learned that there is no fixed distance to travel. You can never say that you have arrived. The goals that you set for yourselves in the early years will soon be achieved, and then new targets will need to be set.

By 1994, we had achieved many of our original goals. We had forged successful customer partnerships and tailored our manufacturing process to our customers' requirements. We had substantially reduced our stocks and work in progress. Our teams were now multi-skilled, and empowered to play a full role in the development of the company. Restrictive job descriptions had been abolished. Our supply-chain partnerships, with our annual hours production capability, had given us amazing flexibility to respond to our customers' unpredictable needs. We were regularly achieving our performance targets of on-time delivery and quality. And so came the question: what next? What indeed?

In 1995 we fixed our sights on continuing to set new and even more challenging targets, to move the goal posts even further apart. What we have learnt is that measurement is the key, and we continue to measure everything. Thus, we decided that we needed a structure for continued improvement and a measurement tool to see just how good we really were. Wonderful affirmations like 'We intend to be the best' or 'We need to do better' we considered as mere sloganising, and we have now adopted the British Quality Foundation's Business Excellence Model as our improvement tool.

This model is Europe's answer to the Baldridge Award, which provides recognition and inspiration for world-class companies. Companies submit a written application to a panel of judges, who then assess the applicant against a model company. Assessment touches every area in great depth.

In the UK, we now have the UK Quality Award, which was first awarded in November 1994. One of the strengths of the model is that for the first time there is a clear and meaningful definition of Total Quality. This is very helpful indeed, since Total Quality seems to mean different things to different people. We talk to companies who say: 'Oh yes, we're doing Total Quality. We really sorted out our marketing department/ despatch area / goods in!', etc. It all goes to show how easy it is to go off at a tangent on project-orientated activities and to lose sight of the whole picture. Unfortunately, with most projects, a problem solved in one area of the company often means problems created elsewhere.

This is where two of the Award's other strengths lie. The model is a self-assessment tool, and it makes you look at your organisation holistically and work logically towards long-term goals. If you want to improve your company, you need to measure where you are now, set goals and keep measuring periodically to sustain the improvements.

The Business Excellence Model

Leadership 10%	People manage-ment 9%	Processes 14%	People satisfaction 9%	Business results 15%
	Policy and strategy 8%		Customer satisfaction 20%	
	Resources 9%		Impact on society 6%	

Enablers	Results
<--><------------------------->	
50%	50%

Figure 56

To enable us to use the model to its full potential, we sent a member of our management team on an Assessor Training Course for the model, and we can now use in-house expertise without needing to bring in consultants.

In the model, 50 per cent of the points are awarded for 'Enablers' and 50 per cent are for 'Results'. A perfect company would score 1,000 points, with the scoring weighted by the various percentages shown in Figure 56. The nine basic categories are further broken down into clearly defined subcategories.

The first thing to note is the results section. Many companies are obsessed with financial performance, which can tend to lead to an attitude of short-termism. The model recognises that profitability can come only from *Satisfying the customer*, which gets 20 per cent of the score criteria. *Business results* accounts for only 15 per cent, and in fact not all of that is concerned with bottom-line profitability. Equally important are factors such as *Increasing your market share, Opening new export markets,* etc.

When we first saw the model (Figure 56), with its clearly laid down definitions of what is expected of a model company, it came as no great surprise to us to see the importance attributed to customer satisfaction. A strong customer focus has always been, after all, one of the main planks of our own quality strategy. But a close examination made us think again. How, we asked ourselves, were we measuring customer satisfaction? The simple truth was that we were not.

So, for the first time ever, we conducted an extensive customer survey, and, being subcontractors, as opposed to original equipment manufacturers, we focused on measuring every single aspect of our company's service performance.

We deliberately kept the body of the questionnaire fairly simple, with tick boxes for the customers to indicate how satisfied they were with various aspects of our company. There were also sections for the customers to offer improvement ideas. The topics addressed were quality of communication, quality of information, and quality of employee attitude. We also had a vital section which asked questions like: 'What extra services would you like Dutton to offer?' and 'What are your goals for the future?'. We wanted to discover our customers' future needs so that we could plan our own strategy to meet those needs.

Various members of the Dutton team carried out the surveys on our customers' premises and got involved in discussions with their peers. It was very interesting to see the different areas that were considered as priorities for our customers. Managing directors talked about growth and

acquisitions; designers talked about technological developments; stores people wanted bigger labels, and so on.

Overall, we were very pleased to find our performance
satisfactory across a whole range of areas, and we were
equally challenged by the new requirements that emerged.
The most important thing for us was future planning, and
here our customers told us quite clearly that they wanted a
one-stop shop – from design to manufacture. This caused us
to shelve ideas for the new computer numerically controlled
presses and robotic welding equipment. Instead, we invested
our money in a sophisticated design facility so that we could
indeed offer our customers the one-stop shop they said they
were looking for. We also formulated an action plan to
address the other key areas identified for improvement.

Then we started to explore the quality model in more
depth, and the second results criterion we addressed was
employee satisfaction. Over the previous few years we had
conducted surveys benchmarking ourselves against Crosby's
criteria in his famous book *Journey to Excellence*. The new
model pointed us towards new aspects, and so we undertook
a completely new employee survey. To make sure the
employees all felt part of it, we ensured that everyone
contributed to compiling the questions, many of which
involved us in taking a long, hard look at our attitudes and
expectations.

The results showed that there were a number of areas of
dissatisfaction, and so we drew up an action plan to address
them. For example, we had focused so hard on team building
and equality of status that we had overlooked the necessity
for some kind of recognition of individual excellence.
However, once you identify an area for improvement, it is
relatively easy to solve, and solve it we did.

The model is particularly useful in pointing out what an

exemplar company would do, and it is always helpful to have a goal to go for. Below is a resume of some of the basic principles of the model.

Enablers (How you do things)

Leadership

The model recognises how crucial a contribution good leadership makes. The purpose of senior management is to set the vision and to cascade that vision effectively throughout the organisation. Processes need to be put into place to enhance communication and provide channels for ideas, planning, review and for action teams. Leadership and commitment to Total Quality need to be sincere and sustained. Leadership must be highly visible, both within the organisation and extending out to customers, suppliers and to the business community as a whole.

Strategy planning

A quality organisation should not be preoccupied with fire-fighting problems or looking over its shoulder in order to stay one jump ahead of the competition. It needs to know what its goals are for 12 months, two years, and five years. Those goals should be based on what the customer is likely to require – and then something more besides.

The strategy needs to be holistic, and the planning process itself needs to involve people at all levels of the organisation. These are the people who will have to make the plan work. It is no use the chief executive having an inspired idea in the bathtub one night if everyone else in the organisation thinks he is next for the men in white coats. New ideas should be brainstormed, discussed, agreed by consensus, and based on good quality data.

People management

As I mentioned elsewhere, people are our greatest asset, and the model shows us how to release their full potential. Team working, empowerment, recognition – all these are key components of a successful human-resource strategy.

Resources

Every organisation has resources, but many are not utilising them to their full potential. Supply-chain partnerships are key aspects here, enabling you to keep stocks low while retaining the ability to respond swiftly to customer needs. Plant and equipment need to be looked at differently. Effective management is not simply a matter of keeping machines busy; it also involves creating the kind of organisation where production operatives can, and wish to, play a major role in preventative maintenance planning and in getting the best out of existing equipment, rather than buying new.

Another key resource is the data and information in the organisation. Processes need to be designed to ensure that data is collected and managed effectively and is available to personnel on a timely basis. Even a company producing an excellent product will struggle if its computer system continually ties it up in knots.

Processes

ISO 9000 addresses company processes very well; but this element represents a mere 14 per cent of the quality model. Clearly, we need to understand fully what our basic business processes are. Many of the things companies do every day – processing orders, sending out quotations, answering enquiries, etc. – are dealt with on a fairly ad hoc basis. By stepping back to take an overall view of our business processes, we can inspire some remarkable re-engineering.

There are many tools for process management, and we have found statistical process control especially useful for production line operations. Processes should aim to fulfil customer requirements while keeping efficiency to the optimum. And the role of Administration is to support the basic business processes, rather than to drive them.

Results

Customer satisfaction

As I have emphasised above, it does not matter how good you are – what matters is how good your customers perceive you to be. The only way to discover this is to go out and ask them.

Customer surveys and market research are essential tools in allowing you to assess yourselves. Customer partnerships also have a key role to play here, encouraging proactive involvement in continuous improvement. Service organisations should look at establishing an effective customer care programme.

Employee satisfaction

Any company exhibiting good practice in terms of the 'Enablers' criteria will naturally score well in the 'Results' section. We all understand the kind of problems experienced by companies with a demotivated, unhappy or frustrated workforce. Staff turnover goes up; morale goes down. Efforts aimed at improvement are largely ignored or are actively blocked.

The model shows us that top-flight companies provide an environment in which both individuals and teams can flourish, grow and make a real contribution. Employee satisfaction surveys are an excellent tool for measuring and identifying areas for improvement. But be warned, only conduct an employee survey if you are prepared for two things: first, to hear some answers that you might not want to hear; and second, once you know the truth, you must be prepared to act. Asking and then doing nothing about the answers is worse than doing nothing at all.

Impact on society

This is a criterion that often causes companies the greatest difficulty. This section seeks to examine your organisation and its interaction with the local community. Issues might include environmental pollution or noise, and what your business actually gives back to your local area.

In our case, we have had very strong links with the community over a number of years, particularly with local schools and colleges. Students at all levels are welcomed into the company for work experience or to do study projects. Our managers visit schools to create those vital school-industry links, and the company itself shares its best practice ideas with others through the Department of Trade and Industry's *Inside UK Enterprise* scheme, as well as through networking activities with other local companies via the local supply-chain network group – via CLASP, our local supply-chain networking group, and other organisations.

Business results

This is the area where shareholders sit up and take an interest. Factors such as profitability, return on assets, and cash-flow management are of course very important. However, they are not the holy grail of business excellence. Besides these areas, the model also directs us to look at non-financial measures of success, such as improving on-time deliveries or opening new export markets. The model actually identifies nine criteria and tackles each in depth, with areas of activity clearly defined.

The scoring process itself is well-defined and logical. It must be used carefully, with full employee participation in the assessment process and in the improvement plans. Otherwise, it might be perceived as merely another management stick to beat the staff with.

The scoring, whether conducted by outside assessors or by company personnel, is a truly positive process. The feedback report shows strengths which the company can build on and areas for improvement, and I believe that we will see many more companies adopting the model as a self-assessment tool. I also hope that many more will have the courage and the ambition to enter the competition itself. It was rather disappointing that at the 1994 award ceremony no small company employing under 250 people was deemed worthy of winning the award. This, of course, in itself makes the award all the more valuable and worth winning.

And so to Dutton's future. We have set a three-year strategy, and are using the model as a self-assessment tool. We completed our first self-assessment in the form of the 75-page submission document in the middle of 1995. The score we achieved will be our first milestone, and it is our ambition to be good enough to enter for the award within a few years.

9

How You Know You Are On The Right Track

Throughout the previous chapters, we have seen how our company has moved from the traditional way of employing people to a new way. We and our team members have changed our values to focus on more positive and rewarding ways of doing things. Even if we, at Dutton, no longer behave in this way, the days of treating employees like mushrooms – keeping them in the dark and feeding them on manure – are regrettably still very much alive in large tracts of British industry and commerce. The question that keeps gnawing at me is: If these attitudes prevail, can we really hope to get all employees to focus on customer needs?

We have seen how the pension industry has yet to recover fully from its policy of paying its sales staff on commission alone. Commission sales mean that staff know that, if they do not sell, they will be unable to pay their mortgages or to eat properly. Such systems often force sales people to go all out to sell at any cost. But, as we have seen only too recently, costs are not always financial. Among the costs might even be the good name of your company. You could end up with a set of thoroughly-antagonised customers, who feel rail-roaded into buying something they do not want. A number of large, well-known insurance companies are now harvesting the results of letting battalions of commission-hungry salesmen onto the streets selling pensions.

Why have I selected this example? Because every single one of your employees is in fact a salesperson for your company, and they cannot be expected to perform to the very best of their abilities if they neither have a stake in its success nor know how their company is doing in the market place.

Traditional British management style tends to work on the premise that insecurity makes people work better. In my view, the opposite is true. Insecurity may make people work harder in your company for short-term objectives, but it will undoubtedly damage your long-term effectiveness.

If people feel insecure, why should they be expected to feel genuine commitment to anything outside their immediate personal and family interest? Shouldn't employees also be recognised as having a stake in the company and be encouraged to take an interest in how it is doing? The shareholders may have more at stake in terms of cash, but the employees rely on their salaries to pay their mortgages, feed their families and enjoy their current standards of living. If employees feel part of a company and know that it is profitable, they should also come to feel that their jobs are that little bit more secure. Such feelings of security allow them to perform more effectively and, should the company hit a difficult patch, as our example shows, they are all the more likely to get actively involved in helping it to survive.

Managing for Success

To be successful, the manager of today must be a leader, a coach and a facilitator. But what exactly is leadership?

In the past, leadership tended to be seen as the preserve of a few exceptional people for whom it was second nature, or of the few who were able to develop those elusive skills. For the most part, you either had it or you didn't. This 'it' often meant social standing, rank or position, often by virtue of birth or because of one's contacts. Furthermore, if you had 'it', the last thing you did was to share it. Your role was to tell people what to do, and of course how they should do it in the most minute detail. You were the guardian, on behalf of your masters, of the body of knowledge and information, all of which was of course strictly confidential. And, in order to carry out this obligation, you operated a very strict chain of command and control. This certainly led to some wonderful empire building, but I am unsure as to where in this equation the external customers came in.

The above scenario left behind over-managed but under-led organisations. The world has changed and management must change, too.

The managers of the present and the future must be true leaders, moving away from the autocratic role to one of being trustees of all the resources that are placed at their disposal. I know from my own experience that it is very hard to let go of the reins and empower your colleagues – to relinquish those controls given to you as a right. In my view, to lead nowadays involves being influential, gaining people's trust, respect, and more importantly their commitment.

Management is about building knowledge through educating and training people, developing effective teams, and organising people to work well together to achieve targets and goals that they have ownership of. This, in turn, will provide tremendous satisfaction and fulfilment for all those involved.

What other skills do the new leaders require? They must be orchestral conductors, developing, nurturing and encouraging their team players. They must be able to understand what makes people tick, and have considerable moral insight. They must be able to introduce a team approach that encompasses their own role and that permeates throughout the whole company, in such a way that both the most and the least able in the organisation are viewed as valued members of the team, and are treated as such.

At Dutton, our team leaders are people who have proven leadership skills rather than the most outstanding technical skills. Technical skills can both be bought in and acquired through training. These people were not originally employed by the company for their leadership potential. It only became apparent later, as they were working closely alongside the others. Thus, Dutton has created and developed a company where leadership skills can and do blossom.

And what has now become the role of the Senior Executive? It has changed. Now, it is to set out the vision; to be the financial trustee; to keep abreast of the twists and turns of the competition; to seize hold of the opportunities; and then to make available the resources necessary to exploit those opportunities. The role is one of a coach, bringing diverse groups of people – people from different social and cultural backgrounds, with differing skills, experience, outlooks and political opinions – to a position whereby they are all pulling in the same direction and working to the same objectives, teaching them how to run their own shows.

So, what qualities do we need as managers and coaches? A coach should be able to ensure that people give of their best, bringing all of their talents to the party. A coach should be able to create the kind of culture and environment in which people can work in multi-functional, self-managed teams, and perform continuous improvement as a natural and everyday activity. A coach must continually reaffirm the goals of the organisation and identify what needs to be done, directing the resources and skills so that the tasks can be accomplished. And, perhaps, one of the most important tasks is to get everyone to understand just how clever they really are, so that they actually do believe that they can and will achieve what is required.

Achieving all this is quite a task for the Chief Executive. Like the other changes discussed, none of this is a quick fix. However, by adopting this approach you should start to see the firefighting disappearing from your organisation; the 16-hour day that was once required should start to come down to much more manageable levels, and the morale of everyone in the company should start to lift.

If you get to this point, it will already be clear that your organisation will have genuinely undergone some significant cultural change, and the company management structure will be much flatter.

At the beginning, I must warn you once again, the change process is very tough. It can be very bloody and very painful. But you will see that over the years everyone in the company will begin to appreciate the fundamental necessity and inevitability of the change itself.

I personally have been going through this change process for more than 15 years. For me, the pace of change has accelerated over the last six years. I stand before you as a completely re-engineered manager. If you can grasp the nettle, you can be like me. You can succeed in changing your company and in the process truly start to have fun at work.

Afterword

Having recently had the opportunity to visit many companies throughout the UK and abroad, both doing presentations and sharing ideas, I am continually surprised how many of these companies maintain structures that derived from another era.

The book *The Machine That Changed the World* by James P. Womack, Daniel T. Jones and Daniel Roos charts the rise and fall of mass production and how Henry Ford revolutionised the process of producing motor cars. By 1915, modern assembly lines had been fully installed at his Highland Park and output had reached capacity. At that stage, the workforce numbered 7000 workers, many of whom had previously worked on the land or were immigrants and could barely speak English. In fact, over 50 languages were spoken among them. This was some headache. Ford's solution was to divide the work into the simplest of tasks and to ask his operators to do just one thing: to hit a spot and hit it a lot. In the process, decision-making was taken away and given to foremen, supervisors and management.

To my mind, this is the way all too many companies continue to operate, despite the fact that today's issues are not those of Henry Ford and his time. We now have a well-educated workforce of talented and capable people whose aspirations bear no comparison to those of workers from way back when. Gone are the days of the 50s, 60s and 70s, when you could sell whatever you could make. The requirements of today's customers have changed so substantially and their expectations raised so dramatically that the demands placed upon us have altered beyond all recognition.

Our role nowadays is to bring every employee to understand about customer care, so as to solve our customers' problems. For this, we need to create structures which are infinitely flexible.

At Dutton, as holders of ISO 9000 and working towards *Investors in People*, we are obliged to produce a blueprint of our company structure for the examining authorities. And yet, without a doubt, each of our employees would have his or her own particular view of our structure - some 28 differing versions in all. This is because Dutton consists of people who are allowed to make decisions and actually do so. If they can't find a solution to a problem, they know just which of their colleagues will be able to help them. Hence, we have abandoned job descriptions. These just put people into boxes and restrict their ability and power to put their capabilities and talents to full use. In our company, we each acknowledge our own view of how the company is structured and we work accordingly.

This has, of course, necessitated a change in the type of people we need to employ for the present and for the future. We now require people with skills that are quite distinct from those appropriate for earlier times. For instance, a welder in our company needs to be computer literate; to be a good communicator; to be able to discuss with designers; and to understand the internal and external wants and needs of customers (Figure 57).

Figure 57

Many shop-floor staff may feel unwilling to work towards this or may doubt their own capacities to achieve results (although, more often than not, it seems to be the managers who are the greatest doubters). However, I am convinced that this represents the only way forward. With patient coaching, training, and determination on all sides, such a situation is achievable. What I believe we have achieved at Dutton - what has marked us of as special - is to bring decision making back into the actual process of making things. With this has come a steadily improving quality of life for all. This is certainly something well worth changing for!

Some Further Points to Ponder

Imagine you are taking part in of one of those 'role swapping' situations, so popular in training films, whereby you change places for six months with one of your own shop-floor employees on, for example, the production line or on the customer-service desk. Now ask yourself whether you would be satisfied with the hours of work, the terms and conditions, the expectations and the rewards. Would you be enjoying your working life?

If you cannot sincerely answer with a resounding 'Yes', then I would recommend that you give some serious thought to improving the situation.

Equally, next time a member of your senior management team takes a walk around your organisation, particularly on the shop floor, ask yourself why they are doing it. If it is an informal visit to say 'Hello, how are you?' or 'Well done, thank you.', then no problem. If, on the other hand, people are looking apprehensively over their shoulders or have their eyes cast down as if waiting for the sword of Damocles to fall, then you have some very serious thinking to do.

If, furthermore, your employees are not too sure who the person is, then the warning bells should really be ringing;

you are in serious trouble. In such cases, my advice would be: take a long and hard look at how you do things; start changing your corporate culture fast.

Often managers do not take sufficient time to think about what they say in their regular chats with employees. My advice is to avoid questions like: 'Any problems this week?' Almost invariably the answer will be 'No'. Ask them what they are doing, what the team is doing, what they thought of the latest piece of company news. Once the pressure is off and they understand that they are not facing the Spanish Inquisition, they will tend to start using these opportunities to bring problems to your attention.

But remember your role. You are not there to solve the problem. You are there to help them solve the problem for themselves. You are essentially there for one thing only – to empower them to change.

Appendix 1

Draft Proposal for the Implementation of Annual Hours

Annual hours is a system of average working time across a year. Employees are contracted to work a given number of hours over 12 months rather than a specific number of hours per week. In an annual system, hours of work can be varied from week to week in accordance with the business requirement.

Benefits for the Company

The primary motivation is the increase of flexibility offered in terms of the ability to match employee hours closely with our customers' requirements. The implementation of annual hours removes the distinction between the basic working week and overtime. The elimination of premium payments for overtime is therefore another reason for moving to a system of annual hours. We also propose to use this opportunity as part of a wider restructuring package which will include a new payment system, revised grading structures and changes in working practices which will help to develop the team culture in the Company.

Benefits for the Employees

The main benefit for the employees is the greater predictability of earnings. Equal instalments of pay throughout the year, regardless of the number of hours worked in a particular week or month, provide a stable income in place of fluctuations in the level of earnings.

We have taken the overtime worked over the last four years, which shows that an average of 160 hours per employee is worked per annum. We will propose to call these either reserved or banked hours. The Company can use these hours for sickness, absenteeism cover, doctors and dentists, funerals (immediate family), reject and rework, jury service and peak production. Payment for the reserve hours will be included in the annual salary, regardless of whether or not the Company calls on these hours.

The Company is aware of the new EU directive on working time, which was adopted in November 1993 by most European countries *but not* the British Government. The directive in principle provides for a maximum working week of 48 hours on average, including overtime. Employees will normally have *the right* to a minimum daily rest period of 11 consecutive hours *and* a minimum rest period of one day a week.

Why Have Annual Hours?

One of the primary reasons for implementing annual hours is to increase flexibility into the organisation. The ability to vary hours of work across the day, week and month means that we are able to match the hours employees are available to work with production requirements. It is felt that this will reduce the 'P'* Number requirement bookings.

Elimination of Overtime

We should see a productivity improvement as everyone looks to working to eliminate the need to work overtime and to get the work done in the shortest possible number of hours. The strict distinction between basic working time and overtime is eliminated and in this way we are able to match our employees' hours more effectively with demand and help reduce the labour costs associated with overtime payment.

Payroll Administration

It is proposed that employees are paid *once* a month on the 20th of the month. We shall have a much more simplified payroll as no overtime premiums would have to be calculated.

Drawbacks

The organisations looked at by the Company have found very few drawbacks associated with the operation of annual

---

* 'P' numbers represent non-direct production activities, such as driving fork lifts, etc.

hours. In companies where time off is rostered there can sometimes be problems in covering unforeseen circumstances, such as the need for compassionate or extended leave and jury service.

The Employees' Perspective

The majority of employees will gain substantially from working annual hours. We propose to compensate for the removal of overtime by consolidating previous overtime earnings into an annual salary. In some instances, however, for individual employees who previously worked a lot of overtime, total earnings would be lower.

The following example shows how annual hours would be calculated:

Basic working week ....39 hours
Working day ....7.8 hours
Annual holidays ....25 days
Statutory holidays ....8 days
Gross annual hours: 52 x 39..................2,028 hours
Less holidays: 25 x 7.8............................195 hours
Less statutory days: 8 x 7.8....................62.4 hours
Net annual hours...1,770.6
Banked hours ....(160)

It is proposed the salary should be £14,500 per employee. The Group Leaders would be paid an additional bonus for the responsibilities they hold. This would eliminate the unfairness voiced to the management on the Company's pay structure. Group members would have to be more flexible in their approach to the tasks they undertake. This lays a responsibility on the management to train people for these new tasks.

Financial Benefits to Dutton

We would expect a productivity increase as people endeavour to complete the work and gain more leisure time.

The Company must look to continue to expand its business and the above will give us a much more competitive position. I would expect our cost rates to drop further, which will affect our hourly selling rate. The management will give all employees an assurance that we will not overload them, but with the existing good communications and further improvements in the area of team working we must expect everyone to buy into the expansion of the Company as this will improve their bonus opportunities and security of employment.

Appendix 2

Dos and Don'ts of *Kaizen*

Do

- Say 'Why don't I?'
- Personally recognise *Kaizen* improvements
- Do the first *Kaizen* yourself
- Provide lots of training and encouragement
- Keep it simple.

Don't

- Say 'Why don't you?'
- Create barriers or spending limits
- Insist on a financial payback
- Pay out large sums of money for improvements. It is very divisive
- Dismiss an idea just because you don't feel it is worthwhile.

Appendix 3

Successful Team Working

Team working requires:

- Time
- Effort
- Training
- A common goal
- A balance of personalities

  - a leader to set the vision
  - a 'creative' to plan how to achieve the vision
  - a 'doer' to turn plans into reality
  - a 'cynic' to stop the team going off at tangents

- Equality of status tempered with recognition for individual effort.

Appendix 4

The TQM & JIT Joint Implementation Model

This model (set out overleaf) was produced by Ioannis Georgousis at Cranfield University during his research into the activities of several companies, including Dutton, that had embraced the change process.

The authors of this book believe that the model has much to offer other companies embarking on corporate transformation.

Success in this endeavour certainly means mobilising absolutely everybody's skills; but to do this means changing attitudes. And that, fellow chief executives, may also mean, we are sorry to say, changing yours!

We wish you the best of luck.

Appendix 4

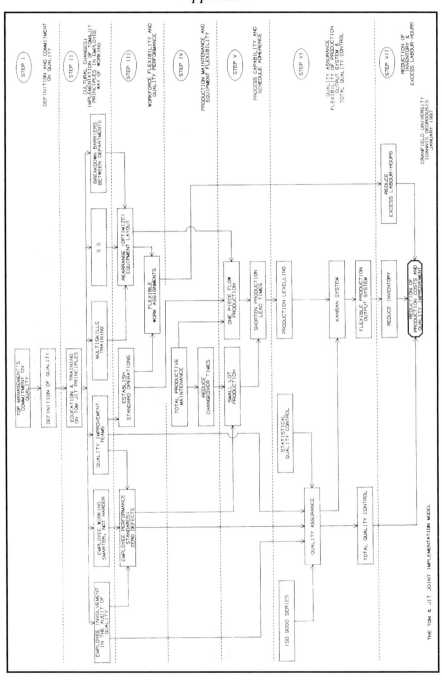

STEP I
DEFINITION AND COMMITMENT ON QUALITY

STEP II
CULTURAL CHANGES: IMPLEMENTATION OF TQM-JIT PRINCIPLES IN EMPLOYEE WAY OF WORKING

STEP III
WORKFORCE FLEXIBILITY AND QUALITY PERFORMANCE

STEP IV
PRODUCTION MAINTENANCE AND EQUIPMENT FLEXIBILITY

STEP V
PROCESS CAPABILITY AND SCHEDULE ADHERENCE

STEP VI
QUALITY ASSURANCE, FLEXIBILITY OF PRODUCTION OUTPUT SYSTEM & TOTAL QUALITY CONTROL

STEP VII
REDUCTION OF INVENTORY & EXCESS LABOUR-HOURS

CRANFIELD UNIVERSITY
IOANNIS GEORGOUSIS
JANUARY 1997

THE TQM & JIT JOINT IMPLEMENTATION MODEL

TOP MANAGEMENT'S COMMITMENT ON QUALITY

DEFINITION OF QUALITY

EDUCATION & TRAINING ON TQM-JIT PRINCIPLES

QUALITY IMPROVEMENT TEAMS

EMPLOYEE INVOLVEMENT IN THE AUDIT OF QUALITY

EMPLOYEE WORKING SMARTER, NOT HARDER

EMPLOYEE PERFORMANCE STANDARDS: ZERO DEFECTS

MULTISKILLS TRAINING

ESTABLISH STANDARD OPERATIONS

BREAKDOWN BARRIERS BETWEEN DEPARTMENTS

5 S

REARRANGE (OPTIMIZE) EQUIPMENT LAYOUT

FLEXIBLE WORK ASSIGNMENTS

TOTAL PRODUCTIVE MAINTENANCE

REDUCE CHANGEOVER TIMES

SMALL LOT PRODUCTION

ONE PIECE FLOW PRODUCTION

SHORTEN PRODUCTION LEAD TIMES

PRODUCTION LEVELLING

STATISTICAL QUALITY CONTROL

ISO 9000 SERIES

QUALITY ASSURANCE

TOTAL QUALITY CONTROL

KANBAN SYSTEM

FLEXIBLE PRODUCTION OUTPUT SYSTEM

REDUCE INVENTORY

REDUCE EXCESS LABOUR-HOURS

REDUCTION OF PRODUCTION COSTS AND QUALITY IMPROVEMENT

Further Information

Among the British and foreign companies and organisations that have visited Dutton Engineering (Woodside) and benefited from the experience are the Police, the Fire Brigade, various High Street banks, and literally hundreds of businesses, large and small, in both the manufacturing and service sectors.

If you wish to learn more about Ken Lewis's ideas and how he transformed Dutton, or require help or advice in terms of changing your company or organisation, Ken would be delighted to address conferences, participate in presentations to your senior management team, or offer consultancy.

Visits of up to 14 people to Dutton Engineering, including a special half-day presentation, a factory tour and buffet lunch, can also be arranged.

For further details contact:

Steve Lytton
CLASP
10 Regent Street
Finedon
Northants, NN9 5NB
Tel: 01933-681009
Fax: 01933-682522
Email: 100410.2712@compuserve.com

Index